CROSSING THE BAR

CROSSING THE BAR

Eeshaan Mahesh

Delta Book World
New Delhi - 110002

First Published in 2018
ISBN : 978-93-85719-08-0

Published by **Abhishek Goel** on behalf of

Delta Book World
G-4, Prahlad House
4832/24, Ansari Road
New Delhi - 110 002 (India)

Ph. : 011-2328 8140, 2324 5799
E-mail : deltabookworld@gmail.com

Illustrations by Shashi Shetye
English Translation by Mr. V.N.Gupta

PRINTED IN INDIA

Dedicated to

my wife

Bindu Popli

binduartaura.blogspot.com

whose paintings are
a humble effort
to look
through the
mysterious world of nature.

...and heartiest thanks to

Mrs. Anita Sharma
(Principal: SD Public School, Pitampura, Delhi)

with whose initiative and help this novel
got translated into English.

From the heart of translator...

When Mrs. Anita Sharma (Principal, S.D. Public School, Pitampura, Delhi) presented this mythological novel 'Jana tha Ganga Paar' by Eeshaan Mahesh and wished to get it translated by me, I felt amazed as it was a new thing for me. I had never translated any classical novel in English before this, though I had translated many stories for children earlier.

I found the language of the novel quite unalloyed and chaste which I had never tasted before but gradually the words settled in my mind. I felt the pulse of the words and try to do justice to them in English.

I was enthralled by the meaningful purple passages containing lively, interesting and thought provoking dialogues. My joy knew no bounds when I read the dialogue between Urmila & Sumitra imbued with sterling qualities of mind and soul. The handling of the plot of the novel with adroitness, profound and matured thoughts by the author was an additional bonus to me.

I would like to quote a few lines by Alfred Lord Tennyson :

For tho' from out our bourne of Time and Place
The flood may bear far,
I hope to see my Pilot face to face
When I have crost the bar.

-Virendra Nath Gupta

Preface

This novel is the English translation of Eeshaan Mahesh's spiritual novel 'Jana tha Ganga paar'. The novel was originally written in Hindi. The story of this novel is based on the notable legendary episode of Lord Rama and Kevata, the boatman.

The sequence of the story says that Lord Rama along with his wife, Sita and his younger brother, Lakshamana were proceeding towards the forests to fulfill their vow of banishment. There, to cross the river Ganges, they happened to board a boat of a boatman named Kevata. His exceptional character made the whole episode dramatic and mysterious.

When after crossing the river, Lord Rama asked the boatman about the fare that has to be paid for the ride, Kevata, the boatman, simply asks Rama to do the same when he, after his death comes to Rama's Ghat, the final doorstep, then he must take him across that.

This novel has peeped into the mystery of the statement given by Kevata. How could he recognize the fact that Rama was the incarnation of the ultimate; though many sages of that time only recognized Rama as a loyal Prince of King of Ayodhya. Only the seven divine sages considered Rama as incarnation of God.

Bindu Popli

Some Dialogues of Characters from CROSSING THE BAR

- I am first a princess and then a wife. If we lead a more comfortable and more luxurious life than our subjects, we must be prepared to make more sacrifices than they do when time demands.

  - Urmila (Wife of Lakshmana)

- O Lakshmana! You are fortunate enough to get a golden opportunity of rendering service to Shri Rama. You are expected to seek the image of your father in Rama, me in Sita and Ayodhya in the forest.

  - Sumitra (Mother of Lakshmana)

- If a king is in possession of his people's wealth, it is not because he has to spend it lavishly on his own comforts and pleasures of life. That wealth is the heritage of the people of his kingdom. It should be used for the welfare of the masses. It is the imperative duty of a king to see that the money earmarked to the administrative authorities is used only for the good of the public.

- Lord Rama

- A day will definitely come when all, after their demise, will come to your door-step *(Ghat)*. At that time, O my Pilot! Don't forget to identify me and take me across the ocean of life. Nobody else but you can help me get the fruit of my labour.

- Kevat, The boatman

ONE

The chariot was running with its full speed. The spokes of its wheels looked to be revolving in the opposite direction on account of its high speed. They had crossed the boundary line of Kosal District. Their chariot proceeded to move towards the divine river- The Ganga (The river Ganges) after crossing the rivers like Vedshruti, the Gomati and the Syendika.

"O Aryaputra!" Sita asked in a pleasant tone, "We have now crossed umpteen rivers. I have felt a characteristic feature of each. Its fragrance, its surrounding climate, birds and beasts wandering around it, its bathing ghats, greenery on its banks and its dwellers- all are different in form and nature from each other, but it is a pleasant diversity. It is certain that everything has sprung from only one source, yet here they are diverse from each other. What's your view about this feeling of mine?"

"All the wise are unanimous in their opinion," spoke Rama, smilingly.

"Then repeat that unanimous view," said Sita too, smilingly.

"Your feeling is the essence of Nature's profundity. In fact, God has lent a distinctive individuality to each and every animate and inanimate object. Not a single tree is identical in this world. Their leaves, fruit and blossoms are different. Therefore, all these objects cumulatively contribute to the place's climate and fragrance. Just as we people look different from each other at every place, similarly, this vegetative world also creates a novel sight of diversity although it belongs to one and the same source".

"If a sacred tree grows on the bank of the Gomati river, another on the Yamuna's and still another on the Saryu's, what difference does it make if each is at a different place?" asked Lakshmana.

"Let us suppose a traveller passing through Ayodhya enters another kingdom. Then he says that there are people in Ayodhya, and also in this kingdom. But what difference does it make when they belong to the same human species?"

"Why not, there is a difference. Lakshmana of Ayodhya has his own distinctive personality. How can there be another Lakshmana of the same sort? At the most, it may be that he looks like Lakshmana in shape and size", burst out Lakshmana before Rama could say anything else.

"Well, it's good that you yourself have answered your questions," spoke Rama. "Suppose there are thirty thousand people in three states in proportion to ten thousand persons in each state. Just as the people of those three states are different from one another, in the same way, the trees, though belonging to one particular species, will not be identical in any way. It's not acceptable to God to create two things of identical nature. He never makes two things similar to each other. It's a different thing that we ourselves fail to recognize their basic difference on account of our limited knowledge."

"Rama, the Supreme Power, organizes and manages everything. Can He be understood?" Sumantra asked while maneuvering the horses to escape from a big pothole. After crossing it safely, he looked at Rama, expecting an answer from him.

"Only Guru Vishwamitra is the sole authority to answer this question. I am not authorized to answer such critical questions."

"Rama, even if you have the sole right upon things, you don't establish your claim upon them. Then what else can I say now? The inner voice of mine told me that since you were answering the questions of all, why should I lag behind? I should also sail in the same swim. But if you don't want to answer my question, then it's all right."

"Kaka (uncle), even you!" Lakshmana laughed, saying so. "What was the need for you to shoot a decisive arrow over such a petty matter? Had you been a Kshatriya, you could have destroyed your own weapons in vain."

"Nobody can gauge that Infinite. There is no way to know Him. How can an infinitesimal being know the Infinite," said Rama staring at the path.

"One can try to be like Him; but one can't understand Him in the way as one can do grammar rules. He is beyond all rules, beyond all reasons and beyond all senses. He is beyond all these things and that's why He is boundless. His graces are infinite. He is showering all His blessings upon all so that they may become like

Him. But alas! We don't happen to realize the significance of the rain of His blessings. Why? It's due to our vanity and arrogance."

"But why can't we understand God?" Sumantra asked in a voice whetted by curiosity. It was an indication of his unbearable agony. "God knows how many times I tried to know Him! But I got so much fixed in His web that I felt it could have been better if I had not tried to know Him. Why is He inaccessible, Rama?"

"'Knowing' is to be associated with information, and it is the function of one's mind to receive information. Mind is also an integral part of one's life like other biological sense organs. It has its own limits. It can see a distance only to a certain extent and understand things limitedly as a manual weapon, if thrown, covers only a limited distance. When we throw a weapon through some instrument, that weapon yields results much better than a manual one. Man can't see all the segments of this earth; he can't gauge the fathom of oceans and seas, and Kaka, you ask why you couldn't know God. Think yourself if you could know in entirety the Saryu river flowing by Ayodhya, on the bank of which you were born and you spent your whole life. Do you know that this river passing through so many kingdoms might have altered its form and shape, depending upon their geographical conditions? It might have also changed its colour on account of the land of that place. If you're made to stand there and asked which river it is, will you be able to identify it and give the right answer?" Rama looked towards Sumantra.

"It's not possible," Sumantra spoke in a low voice.

"Can a small ant guage the height of the Himalayas?"

"Never."

"Can a small drop of water know an ocean?"

"It's impossible."

"But if that drop of water falls into the ocean, it itself becomes an ocean," Rama smiled.

On hearing this, Sumantra was so bewildered that his mouth gaped wide open.

"The effacement of the drop of water is nothing but the elimination of haughtiness. The drop is an obstacle in itself. But it has another phase too. This also occurs. Sometimes the ocean lets itself fall upon the drop, and the drop gets merged with the ocean. Such a situation arises only when the drop purges itself so much that the ocean feels obliged to rise up from its place to meet the drop. It has to make itself so much attractive that the ocean can't help having a rendezvous with it. The heart of the ocean gets so much vexed that it flounders to assimilate the drop in itself. But, Kaka, the consecration of the drop is often a rare phenomenon. However, we can't deny its possibility. It lies in the form of a seed, and that seed sprouts at such a desolate and lonely place where only God can notice it or those, who are godly and angelic, are moving about in their mortal coil."

Sumantra kept on looking at Rama as if gulled by him. He had thought till today that Rama was only a skilled administrator, that he was a meek and precocious prince who could run the administration in a beautiful way; such a leader who ruffled the hearts of the public when they knew that their Rama had been exiled from Ayodhya. His departure made them feel as if their soul had deserted their body. Up till now he couldn't see Rama's grand spirituality. He was so near to him yet he couldn't know who was residing in the innermost being of Rama. Why couldn't he realize that there was something special in Rama, which was lacking in others? He had heard from Maharaja Dashratha that even Parashurama bowed his head before Rama after recognizing him. If any other king had said so, he would have assumed that he was boasting and thereby demonstrating his vanity through the medium of his son or that he was creating an ethos to make his son a popular figure. But he knew Dashratha very well. He knew that the king Dashratha was not a liar. Whatever had actually happened, Dashratha stated as it is in the same way. Then his mind told him that Parashurama was acting in that way out of courtesy or civility, bearing in mind the virtues of Rama, the reputation of an ideal prince and the presence of Guru Vashishtha.

He broached this topic with Dashratha also in order to know its essence. But then Dashratha attached no importance to this context and said that Parashurama was ceaselessly feeling undone by the reasoning power of Rama. Rama knew that in the presence of Guru Vashishtha, Parashurama could do no ungood to him, and so dauntlessly he rendered all the reasonings of Parashurama ineffective. Then, in order to save his honour, he asked Rama to pull the string of his Vaishnavi bow. Thereafter he slunk away, calling Rama a worthy figure. It was the only best way for Parashurama to do so in his withering age. Dashratha had taken the whole episode in a light, comical vein. He hadn't perceived even an atom of divinity in it. By virtue of his intelligence, Sumantra got a chance to have a taste of Dashratha's briefing. He too took Rama only a child who played in his lap and at the most a unique prince. When he couldn't understand even Rama, how could he understand God? He felt that he was the victim of his own self-deception. Rama had truly said that we, on account of our vanity, couldn't realize the value of God's blessings being showered upon us ceaselessly. The Seven Sages said, "Rama! You are the same infinite being." But Rama didn't show any reaction to the declaration of the Seven Sages (*Sapta-Rishis*). Many other ascetics said, "Rama, let the Seven Sages say what they feel like. But we know that you are only a king's son. Then smilingly Rama looked towards those Sages. The eye witnesses say, "This smile of Rama was celestial as well as enigmatic. There were waves of electric current in his smile which fell upon one's soul like a lightning." Sumantra stood aghast. He got mentally disturbed. Today when Rama stepped out of that royal ethos, some fragrance of Rama went into his nostrils. But now it was too late as Rama would desert even him and go into the dense forests. He felt within the heart of his hearts that it was only Rama who could guide him to the path of God. But awaiting the end of fourteen years of Rama's banishment would take away his life. No, he would not return to Ayodhya after bidding good-bye to Rama. Even if Rama ordered him to do so, he would not. He felt that he was on the starting point of knowing Rama a little.

"It seems that Kaka has fallen into the ocean like a drop of water or the ocean itself has fallen upon him," Lakshmana burst into peals of laughter.

Sumantra looked towards Lakshmana, and an idea struck his mind to say, "The ocean itself has fallen upon me. I've risen to consciousness. But when will you rise to?" Just then the inner voice erupted in him. He recognized that it was Rama's voice. It said, "So far as Lakshmana is concerned, he recognized me long back. That's why he didn't take even a moment's time to decide to accompany me, leaving behind his all. Without me everything is like dust for him?" Sumantra failed to understand why it was happening so to him. Was it the result of so many days of fatigue? He controlled himself: 'No, the clouds of doubt in my mind were once again trying to veil the divine incident in my life.'

* * *

Sumantra pulled the reins of the horses. They neighed and lifted their two front legs to indicate they wanted to stop. The chariot swung round and came to a halt.

"Now we are on the banks of the Ganga at Shrungverpur, Shri Rama," said Sumantra, folding his hands and touching his brow with them in full submission.

Rama gazed at the Ganga with reverential looks. It was clear from his gaze and smile that he had heard what Sumantra had said. But he was silent on account of ecstasy aroused by the holy sight of the Ganga. Rama directed his eyes towards Lakshmana and Sita. They too were feasting their eyes upon the beauty of the Ganga with lingering looks.

They all stepped down from the chariot and advanced towards the Ganga bank. Sumantra drove the chariot towards a tree and made it halt under it. He unyoked his horses and started patting them lovingly.

"O Lord! If we had got life-long banishment, it would have been better. If the pitcher had broken, we would have got rid of filling it with water." Touching softly the ripples of the Ganga, Sita greeted it.

Rama and Lakshmana too adoringly greeted the Ganga. "Behold, Lakshmana! Look at the ashrams of ascetics and sages. They are situated on its banks. This flowing Bhagirathi is divided into three streams here. Human beings, gods, demons, nagas, Gandharva, eunuchs and all other beings feel contented when they use the pleasantly cold, holy water of this divine river. On either side of its banks are located numerous mountain ranges and pleasant spots for gods. I salute this divine land. The gardens and orchards on its either side surpass even heavenly gardens in Indralok. When its water strikes against boulders and rocks, it produces a noise which sounds like the wild laughter of the Ganga. Its setting looks like her spotless smile. Somewhere its flow is like a braid of hair and somewhere it becomes circuitous on account of the formation of whirlpools. It looks as if a forest girl were dancing like a pulley or top. Somewhere, where the water is deep, it is calm and quiet and somewhere its speedy flow is producing a terrible noise which sounds like Lord Indra's thunderbolt. Thumping its waves, the wind is creating the sound like that of tom-toms, drums, etc. At certain other places the wind with its fingers is plucking the strings of waves and producing musical sound like the one that comes from a veena, a sitar, a flute and one-stringed instrument. There is a wide stretch of shallow portion of the water to the farthest corner and the scattered boulders of different shapes are lying in it. It looks as if these stones by rolling miles and miles together had shed the rigors of their vanity. It appears that these boulders whipped by the currents of Ganga water have outbeaten the flowers in their tenderness. Lying in the Ganga water for a long duration of time, every stone has turned into a Shivlinga. The lustrous gem-like Ganga has sprung from Lord Vishnu's feet and Neelkantha (Lord Shiva) has borne it on his head. It is, therefore, unpolluted in itself. But at the same time it has the excellent quality of making the impure pure. Its water is curative of many diseases. It provides energy and sustains life for a longer period as it has all the properties of various minerals. The sages have rightly said that Ganga water is a divine nectar."

"Sita Mata! You had better write an original book on the purifying nature of the Ganga for ascetics during the period of exile. It will be good for the welfare of the world." Saying so, Lakshmana plunged into the Ganga and popping his head out, he said, "Har, Har Ganga! Mother Ganga! Tell our Sita Mata that sharks, alligators, crocodiles and many types of serpents also reside in the water. She could depict them also."

"I have left that chapter for you to write on these violent creatures, Lakshmana. You have to complete it". Sita cupped her hands to hold water in them, and threw it at Lakshmana.

This time, instead of plunging into the water, Lakshmana dived into it.

"Lakshmana hasn't yet come out of the shell of his childhood disposition", said Sumantra after coming closer to Rama as if to declare his presence.

"It's good, in a way, Kaka! Let the child nestled in Lakshman's heart remain alive forever. The child who observes nature in amazement rejoices ecstatically. It bounds and skips like a deer. It's an ill-luck of man that he discards his infancy and announces his adulthood very soon. The very moment he bids good-bye to his childhood, he buries into oblivion his softness, chastity, smoothness and simplicity."

Rama looked fascinatingly towards Lakshamana and said to Sumantra, "Look, Kaka! Even now he is conversing with water-edged birds and cranes like a naive child who doesn't know that birds don't understand any human language." Then Rama cast his looks upon Sumantra and spoke lovingly, "O Charioteer! Can you see that multi-branched soap berry tree yonder, the one which is adorned with blossoms and newly sprouted leaves? Tonight we'll take rest in its happy sight."

"This tree is really very beautiful," said Sita who had overheard Rama while coming closer to him.

SHASHI

Directing his eyes towards that place, Rama averred, "Sita! From there we shall be able to catch a glimpse of the beneficial Ganga river branched into rivulets as well as sweeten our ears with the melodious buzzing sound of their folklores".

"I'm going to fetch the chariot here. Why should anyone go to that place on foot?" turned Sumantra to bring it without seeing Rama's reaction. By this time Lakshmana came out in his wet clothes from the cooling effect of Ganga water and appeared on the scene, shivering.

"What would happen if you ran fever because of so many plunges in the river! This is not Ayodhya where a physician appears in no time before you suffer from any disease. Your brother knew that you would create chaotic conditions in the forest. So, he didn't agree to take you with him to the forest," Sita chided Lakshmana. But her scolding was tinged with affection.

"It's the sole function of a mother to scold a child whatever he does. If I hadn't bathed in the Ganga, do you know what you could have said?

You would say that such a long journey was undertaken and the whole body was covered with dust and dirt. Even then he didn't plunge into the Ganga and stay happy and active. It's not your fault because all mothers are like you," Lakshmana spoke out, squeezing his clothes.

The chariot arrived and all occupied their seats in it. It stopped under the multi-branched soap berry tree. It was a solitary tree in the midst of a high mound. It looked like a huge umbrella, an umbrella on which skilled and able painters had adorned it with leaves and flowers. They all alighted from the chariot. Taking it to be a resting place, Sumantra unhitched the horses. Then he along with Lakshmana began to make beds woven with long grass and leaves. Sita picked up the flowers scattered all around. In a short while, a necessary arrangement was made for night-sleep.

"If you permit me to go to the forest, I'll arrange for fodder for horses," Sumantra sought permission.

"Who knows what horses would be thinking that every day they used to get stomach-full nutritious food and today nobody took care of their breakfast even. With whom were they hitched at this most unopportune time?" Lakshamana spoke out aloud so that horses could hear him.

"These creatures don't think so, Prince!" Sumantra laughed.

"How can you say so?" There was a dramatic problem glimpsed in the voice of Lakshamana.

"I can say so because I know these horses very well. These are war horses. These are so powerful and strong that even if they don't happen to get full food for certain days, it wouldn't leave any impact upon their efficiency," Sumantra told him.

"How can you say this also," said Lakshamana in the same style.

"I can say this also because these are trained to live in these adverse circumstances during military exercise. And you too know this. So now they're proving their mettle."

"Fine! Let them prove their mettle. After reaching Ayodhya, you should get a framed appreciation letter from the Maharaja and hang it around each horse," clapped Lakshmana laughingly.

The horses neighed and snorted loudly.

"Just see, the horses have taken it ill!" Sita spoke.

"Didn't take it ill, Ma! They've laughed at what I said," said Lakshmana.

"They've neither taken it ill nor laughed." On seeing the horses neighing, there was a touch of anxiety in Sumantra's voice. "It's an indication of some approaching danger. They're having the premonition of some mounted enemy trespassing our well-guarded area."

Realizing the gravity of the situation and taking into stock the warning given by horses, Lakshmana immediately darted towards the chariot, and in the blinking of an eye, he equipped himself with all arms and weapons.

"Won't you be prepared for the occasion, Aryaputra!" said Sita with a spark of restlessness in her eyes.

"Site! Let there be an occurrence first before

you get worried!" spoke Rama with a smile. "Many days have passed since Lakshmana had a chance of using his weapons. So, he and his weapons are feeling desperate. He is ever ready for a chance that can give him a taste of crushing his enemies."

"But what about the warning of the skilled charioteer, Sumantraji and the horses?" Sita was bewildered at Rama who was taking it all in a light manner. She said, "O My Lord, Rama! You mustn't be so careless."

"O Lord, be careful! See, a horde of the enemy is coming towards us," said Sumantra with a touch of caution in his voice. "I'm also getting ready to face the situation."

"You caress the horses, and get them rid of their restlessness, Kaka. Leave the rest to Lakshmana," feeling quite confident, Rama stood by the tree.

One could see on the way many mounted persons, well-equipped with arms and weapons coming from distance.

"Are you not worried?" Sita came close to Rama and said in a perplexed tone, "How will

Lakshmana be able to face so many enemies all alone?"

"You're looking at him through the eyes of a mother!" Rama smiled.

"And what about you? How are you looking at Lakshmana?" Sita's voice was shaky. She couldn't understand why Rama was taking this awful situation so lightly.

"I'm looking at him as a great warrior. What a kind of warrior is he if he can't make his enemies lick the dust? Anyhow, the coming armed persons aren't our enemies."

"How can you say this?" Sita's vexation increased.

"Such questions are asked by Lakshmana," said Rama light- heartedly.

"You do one thing. Summon Lakshmana and ask him whether he wants Rama's help."

"Lakshmana, I am just sending your brother to you. Don't worry," shouted Sita, giving assurance to Lakshmana.

While looking at the armed persons, Lakshmana addressed Sita at the top his voice,

SHASHI

"Ma, send not only brother Rama but also our great father Dashratha with his army consisting of elephants, horses, chariots etc. And also send the brave Kaikeyi mother with them so that, if we're rendered unconscious by the enemies, she may protect us and then you may give her four vows out of pleasure. It's because the vows given by the revered father were not sufficient."

When Sita heard Lakshmana's sarcasm, she looked at Rama, feeling amazed. Rama was laughing uncontrollably. Sita had never seen him laughing in this style. She couldn't understand what was all this happening. Sumantra was anxious; Lakshmana stood guard. But Rama felt assured as if he were going to witness dance drama in a theatre.

Lakshmana saw that a horde of powerful tribal warriors was advancing towards them. It didn't appear from their style of coming closer that their aim was to make an attack on them. In the rear part of the group were many loaded bullock-carts moving at a snail's pace. The horses were shuffling their feet in a way as if they were coming to honour a guest.

Lakshmana's forehead was now creased with streaks of worries: Since we haven't come here on a state visit, it can't be that any king in the neighborhood will send this party of tribals in our honour. They might be the forest folk or it might be a part of the hypocrisy of demons.

"Stay and stop where you are," Lakshamana's echoed voice had severity by way of warning. "Give your introduction."

The armed mounted persons spoke nothing. They stood aside, leaving the middle path vacant. Behind them appeared the most powerful giant-sized person. He was unarmed and on foot.

"Lakshmana!" he ran towards him with a streak of restlessness in his voice.

It struck Lakshmana that his voice and figure was somewhat known to him. He stepped forward and embraced Lakshmana before the latter could recognize him. With tears in his eyes, he said, "My friend! What crime did I commit that you didn't think it right to inform me about your arrival?"

"Oh! We actually forgot that we had sojourned in Shringverpur, the kingdom of Nishadraja Guha," said Lakshmana, looking at Guha whose eyes were welled up with tears. "Nishadraja! I'd committed not only one mistake of forgetting you but also got prepared for war, thinking that demons were coming. Look! I've in my hand the arrows that will send a person to the Kingdom of Death."

"The person whom Rama forgets has no place even in the Kingdom of Death, my brother!" Guha felt overwhelmed with emotion.

"Lakshmana took him in his arms tightly, and embracingly said, overbrimmed with emotion, "I seek your pardon from the core of my heart, friend! Let's go and meet Shri Rama."

When Rama saw Guha coming closer to him, he spread out both of his arms to embrace him. Overwhelmed with emotion, Guha advanced towards Rama hastily. He somewhat bent. Perhaps he wanted to fall at the feet of Rama. But Rama understood his feelings. The moment Guha bent forward, Rama took him in his arms and clung him to his breast before he insisted on touching the dust of his feet.

"Shri Rama!" saying so, Guha felt choked.

"What ails you, friend!" Rama placed both of his hands lovingly on Guha's shoulders and made him sit on a mat nearby.

"You're the lord of all luxuries of life. It's a heart-rending sight for me to see you in the garb of a hermit. Cast off these clothes and accept my kingdom as the Kingdom of Ayodhya. O Mighty! I welcome you. I've brought with me many a comfortable bed, beautiful clothes of various kinds, delicious royal delicacies and grams and nutritious grass for horses. My kingdom is yours and from today onward you are our lord and we are your serfs. I feel gratified that you're our guest." Guha folded his hands and an ocean of tears flowed from his eyes.

"You rightly dubbed us 'guests'. Our arrival is sudden and accidental. There was no date fixed for our arrival here; so, naturally, we are guests, Nishadraja! And it doesn't behove a guest to encroach upon his host's house and become its owner."

Rama cast his smiling looks upon Guha's very special persons sitting all around him and then said to Guha, "Friend! You've come on foot to me to express your love and affection. This feeling of yours is no less than ever-green worship and hospitality for us. I'm extremely happy to see you, Nishadraja! The friendship of such simple- hearted persons as you're is very dear to me."

"What are you saying, My Lord! It's our good luck that you grant us so much respect, afford us so much love, otherwise we stand nowhere before your kingdom and might. Very petty kings look down upon us because we're not the segment of Kshatriya society. Nor do we have the military powers as they have. But you never let us feel all this." There was a sense of gratitude in Guha's voice.

"See, friend! Try to understand the essence of things. Never underestimate yourself. But it never means that you grow vain and consider yourself greater than others as the so-called 'high-caste' vain people do. I mean to say that it's not good to take yourself to be a 'demeaned' man and suffer from inferiority complex. Your very existence is complete in itself. As a matter of fact, everyone's whole being is complete in itself. If a grass flower thinks that in comparison to a vast lotus flower how small it is, it means that that flower is disregarding nature and God. The importance of a flower lies in its blossoming. Its value is in blossoming. Not to try to blossom and remain half-blossomed is a sign of one's carelessness. There is no kind of discrimination when a blossomed flower gives us joy. In nature everything is beautiful. Maybe, in the calculation of man, some are beautiful and many others are ugly. All blossoms in nature are equal. None is great or small on the grounds of colour, size or species. Hence we should not attach any importance to the feeling of discrimination in our heart on account of some ignorant, vain and unknowledgeable persons." Rama's voice echoed from beyond.

"Then please accept all the goods brought by me for you." Guha folded his hands in full submission.

"Accepted, and now you are ordered to take

back all the things accepted by me and distribute among your friends and realtion." Noticing a shadow of sadness on Guha's face, Rama said assuringly, "Friend, otherwise I would've taken them all. But this time I am bound by my vows. In such a situation I'm dependent on clothes made from bark of trees, deer skin and food provided by the forest. I hope you're trying to understand the value of my vows."

"But accept at least something, my Lord!" Insisted an old man who had accompanied Guha.

"I accept the food brought for the horses. Their mere contentment will amount to the hospitality shown to me. These horses are very dear to my father. Whatever you provide to them, take it for granted that you've given to me." Rama looked towards Sumantra and spoke, "Your wish is fulfilled, Kaka!"

"It's the time for your evening prayer. Till then I along with Kaka will look after the horses." They all understood what Lakshmana meant and came down from that mound.

Guha sent back some of his servants who had come with him. He instructed some of them to stay around half a mile away from Shri Rama's resting place and appointed the most selected bodyguards to keep vigil from a place sufficiently away from the mound.

"Nishadraja! How did you come to know that we're here? You've brought all these things in such a short time and in such an orderly arranged way that it means you'd a prior information of our arrival here," asked Lakshmana, patting the horses who were enjoying the mixed nutritious food of grams, etc.

"No prior information but a sort of premonition. My secret agents informed me that Shri Rama's chariot would move towards Shringverpur. So I conjectured that you would all accept my hospitality," Guha looked towards the horses admiringly. He had never seen so healthy and so strong horses in his life.

"Then what was the need for loading the bullock-carts with goods?"

Lakshmana looked smilingly at Guha slantingly.

"Are you trying to entrap me in your logic?" laughed Guha.

"I know this also that Shri Rama had neither entered any other kingdom's boundary line nor had he informed anyone about his arrival. I apprehended that he might cross even my kingdom's boundary line without informing me. In that case, I would have been very unfortunate. It was the grace of gods that a good sense prevailed over me and I remained alert and was able to present myself in front of my Lord on his arrival."

"Then come friend! Let's go to the service of Rama. His evening prayer might have been over". Lakshmana cast his arms around the neck of Guha. Swinging like a child, relieved from worries, he and Guha moved towards Shri Rama. At that time Rama was lying on the mat interwoven with grass and leaves. Sita was sitting beside him and discussing something. Rama sat up when he saw Guha.

"Kaka has arranged for some sweet fruits of the forest. Let me fetch them," said Lakshmana.

"You fetch me only Ganga water. I'll drink it and take rest," said Rama.

"Yesterday also you took only Ganga water and today..."

With a gesture of his hand, Rama signaled to Lakshmana to keep quiet.

"I'll also drink only Ganga water," spoke Sita.

"All right! I'll take the entire food brought by Nishadraja and spend the whole night in taking it, and stay awake," Lakshmana thumped the ground with his feet like an angry child and went away for Ganga water.

"Brother Lakshmana hasn't changed at all. He is still the same as he was. He is the one who lives in the present. If he is annoyed now, he'll remain annoyed. But the next moment he doesn't remember what provoked him. From his outward conduct, an ordinary person will think that he's a stone-hearted person," spoke Guha when he saw Lakshmana running towards the Ganga.

"Who can assess from the outward

semblance of the sea that an unshaken, quiet spirit resides in the depth of the ocean - the one that always remains unaffected by its waves," Sita endorsed the words of praise spoken in favour of Lakshmana.

"Nishadraja! Are the people of your kingdom well? I hope under your suzerainty they will be living happily and feeling safe and sound under your protection," Rama changed the topic. "Anyhow, beware of your foes in and outside your kingdom."

"Enemies from within?"

"Beware of the evils enshrined within you. Vanity, jealousy, envy, hatred, greed, fear, etc. are more ferocious. They're adept in disguising themselves. Therefore, keep a vigil over them very carefully. You are the sovereign of your people. You have to bless your life-long journey by upbringing your subjects as a father looks after his children. I know you're on the righteous path. But if I'm saying all this to you, it's because it's my duty as a friend of yours."

"I've no knowledge of what is ethical or unethical, what is right or wrong! I'm only following in your footsteps. You're my model. You're my creed. I seek my welfare in your love and graces," Guha bowed his head before Rama.

* * *

Rama and Sita were sleeping together, quite contented on the mats of leaves. Lakshmana was awake and stood guard. Guha was also sitting with him and had been gazing at him for a long time.

"Lakshmana, I perceive that you're plunged in some deep thought. Is it only a spark of doubt in me or what I'm thinking is right?" Guha asked him when he could no longer resist himself.

"What you're thinking is right. I'm besieged by doubts.

"What sort of doubts?"

"It's a riddle, more than a doubt."

"What is it?"

"Maharaja Dashratha, our father, was blessed with an elder son, Rama after the successful performance of many religious rites.

This Ayodhya became more prosperous than a paradise because of the graces of Shri Rama. It will always remain an insoluble riddle for me how Maharaja Dashratha abandoned Ayodhya and his own pedestal," Lakshmana persisted,"I believe that since Shri Rama has forsaken Ayodhya, the condition of our father must have been very deplorable. He might have left his mortal coil. The same condition might Mother Kausalya have been in. She also might have been floundering like a fish out of water when she was bereft of Shri Rama, her only strength and staff or she would bid good-bye to this world, thinking that her life was now meaningless. How ardent was the wish of Maharaja to make Rama ascend the royal throne! But since his wish was not fulfilled, he was ready to forsake his life, repeating the words "Alas! I'm completely undone!" He felt that his life was colourless and substanceless".

"But why do you feel so? Maharaja Dashratha is a great Kshatriya. He is capable of bearing all such kicks of destiny." There was a sense of solace in Guha's voice, " When I heard that Shri

Rama was paying the price for Maharaja's vows, I, like all others, didn't hesitate in cursing him whole-heartedly. But when I knew that Shri Rama didn't speak ill of his father even once for his deed, I lost the pinch of pain. On the other hand, Shri Rama called his father an epitome of truth and ethicality. He took it to be his prime duty to honour his father's vows and renounced that vast and prosperous kingdom happily and immediately. In his lust for kingdom man otherwise makes ceaseless efforts and hatches plots. So, you shouldn't take it to your heart, and feel aggrieved. By this time your father might have become normal and will be busy in making Bharata ascend the throne of Ayodhya in the royal assembly."

"No, friend! You don't know my father. There are three types of people in this world. First, there are those who have lust for wealth and money. In their eyes, nothing else but wealth has its importance. They want to grab it by hook or crook. In their greed to get it quickly, they follow the evil path. By means of injustice, cruelty, exploitation and corruption they heap wealth. Only money is the be-all and end-all of their life. You might have heard that many traders or well-reputed and honourable persons commit suicide when they lose their wealth. They think that once wealth is lost, everything is lost. Such persons are mean and base."

"And what about the second type?" Guha thought that he could not get a chance to have a talk on such knowledge-related subjects with Shri Rama, so he established my contact with Lakshmana. Naturally, he would get its full benefit.

"The second type of people are those who want both material wealth and honour. For them wealth and respect are like the two wheels of a chariot that move side by side. If either of them gets destroyed, their life becomes disease-ridden and burden to them. Then the one wheel of the chariot-life doesn't move without support. It stumbles and gets ruined."

"What are these types of people called?"

"They're called the average type of people."

"And what about the third type?"

"The people belonging to the third type are real human-beings. They are true human-beings. The rest are the animals of flesh and blood in the garb of a man. These people of the best category live only for their principles, honour and values of life. If money misses their life, it makes no difference. Why don't you take the case of Shri Rama? When Kekai talked about banishment, do you know what Shri Rama said in reply, quite feeling undisturbed?"

"What did he say?" Guha's mouth opened and his eyes dilated in amazement as he was curious to hear those words.

"He said: Your Ladyship! I don't want to lead my life as a mammon of money and wealth in this world. Like ascetics I've taken refuge only in leading an austere life. I'll do every task assigned to me by my revered father even at the cost of my life. Take it for granted that I've fulfilled my father's wish. There is no pious duty for me other than carrying out his order and wish. Although father hasn't even once told me about Bharata's ascendency to the royal throne and the banishment of mine for fourteen years yet I'm prepared to spend the days of my life in a deserted forest if you simply breathe out so."

"Though he is deprived of the entire wealth and property yet he is happy because the pure blood of ethicality and constraints has been flowing in his veins, keeping him healthy. Similarly, the main principle of our father, Maharaja Dashratha's life is: dedication to truth; to safeguard the truth. Whatever he is, he is otherwise afraid of doing any unethical work. If by sheer ignorance he happens to commit any immoral act, he feels tortured by agony and suffers from untold sufferings on becoming conscious of the evil deed. After being the victim of defamation from all directions, ill-reputed and degrading words of his wives, and having fallen from the scale of the eyes of his people and personal attendants, he won't remain alive because the foundation of his life is self-esteem."

"Then it means that if those guiltless who belong to the best category of men are held guilty, they die of agony," asked Guha.

"No. If they're innocent or faultless, and howsoever the world charges them with guilt, howsoever it defames them, they remain unshaken because they know that they've done nothing wrong. It becomes a deplorable state of affairs only when they fall from the scale of their own eyes. Whether the world honours or dishonours them, it doesn't make much difference. Only one thing makes difference, and it's when they do such an act as makes them feel ashamed of looking at their own image in the mirror." Lakshmana looked at Guha, " The persons of the best category have always to be alert and vigilant."

"And what about your mother Sumitra? Didn't she feel hurt and aggrieved? But why didn't you express your anxiety about her?" Guha tried to corner Lakshmana, "How can you shut your eyes upon her sufferings?"

"My mother!" Lakshmana laughed. "When I see her, I'm reminded of the poets who have written their poems in praise of the brave lady Kshatriyas, and I endorse what they've written. They are ruled by a sense of duty and don't allow any other feeling to intercept it. If, by mistake, any firefly of irresponsibility strikes them, their sense of responsibility burns it in its flames. Besides this, she is assured that Shatrughana will control the situation. And it's curious that nobody else thought of it.

"And your spouse?"

"She also belongs to the same category. It's really cumbersome to understand such characters." There was a sense of pride in Lakshmana's voice, "I know that the people of this mundane world will say that I did a great injustice to Urmila and she, the innocent and detached- had to bear all sufferings. It makes me laugh when I ask myself why the common masses use such insulting words instead of honouring us. I got inkling from somewhere that Shri Rama, Sita, I and Urmila are irrational and detached people."

"But why does it happen so? Why don't the common people understand the greatness of exceptional people?" asked Guha in a low voice.

"How will you understand when the sense of wisdom is limited? How will it be able to peep through the unlimited? Haven't you heard the story of a frog in a well? Howsoever you may make it understand that there is a water body called an ocean, which is endlessly many times vaster than this well, it can't be made to understand. In its eyes, the size of the sky is only that much as it looks to one from the outside round edge of the well." There was an assimilation of zest in the voice of Lakshmana. "This action of Shri Rama is an index of stupidity in the eyes of the people who are greedy of money. Every person first places himself in that state and then evaluates. It seems to him that when he is prepared even to lose his life for the sake of a little benefit, how it is that Rama has forsaken a limitless treasure of wealth. On the mental plane he thinks of Rama to be an immature, irrational creature and Urmila, the poor woman who has been sacrificed at the altar of their foolishness. How does he know that beyond this body there are certain values of life, which reinforce the spirit of such people? I know that Urmila will never breathe out even a single word in this context throughout her life. She has thrown herself into the flames of her responsibility. If a person surrenders himself or herself to the fire of austerity, it is the emergence of pride, and not of trouble. The only remedy to understand its level is only to be wedded to this level. Only those who are immersed in Shri Rama can understand him or the great Rishis blessed with divine eyes."

"Lakshmana! Why did you decide to accompany Shri Rama?" Guha looked at Lakshmana and said laughingly, "Don't you think that it's a stupid act of yours from the view-point of an ordinary person like me. I simply want to know the feelings behind your decision. I don't think that you took this decision out of unthoughtful excitement or that you don't understand the implication of fourteen years of exile!"

"I can't think of a life without Shri Rama. I owe him my devotional love. It's my good luck that Shri Rama is my elder brother - I got him, so easily. I am ready to sacrifice many mortal coils and many lives, and not one body and one life only for his sake. I can see clearly that the same Supreme Being is expressing His inexplicable divine deeds through the body of Shri Rama." There was divinity in Lakshmana's voice.

"This is exactly what I wanted to say, Lakhan! The forest itself is my kingdom, and so I'm lucky enough to touch the sacred dust of the feet of sages and ascetics quite often."

"Many ascetics began to say that the eldest son of King Dashratha of Ayodhya is the incarnation of Shri Hari Himself." Saying so, the eyes of Guha moistened and he spoke in a hoarse voice, "By truth nobody else but Rama is dear to me in this universe. He is the most beloved of mine. It's only by his grace I long for religious, economic, physical activities and salvation too in this world. Whatever I have got till now is only by his grace. And Lakshmana, it's because of you he is enjoying sound slumber now. If you hadn't come with him, Shri Rama would have to remain awake for the protection of Sita."

"You're giving airs to my vanity. I'm already

suffering from no less vanity. What powers do I have that I could protect the Lord of Three Worlds? These are his divine activities that I'm witnessing. The completion of any work is only due to his grace. Fame he gives only to his servant. He didn't first agree to take me with him. He put such conditions before me that once I thought it was a beautiful strategy of Shri Rama to reject me. But later I realized that he is far-sighted. What we fail to see is all seen by his divine sight. He is the one who can see the past, the present and the future. He is far from all illusions. An illusion can't touch him. It waits as a maid-servant to receive his orders. Shri Rama is the master of all illusions."

"What were those vows?" There was a supplication, an urge in the voice of Guha to hear that context.

"One was to give the kingdom of Ayodhya to Bharata and…"

"I'm not talking about him. Now the whole world knows this," Guha broke in.

"Then what kinds of promises?"

"Those which Shri Rama placed before you in order to permit you to accompany him."

"Oh! Nishadraja! You forget nothing!" Lakshmana laughed.

"Firstly, Shri Rama adopted many strategies not to let Mother Sita accompany him."

"But the revered Sita is your sister-in-law. But have you been addressing her as 'Ma' from the very first day?" Guha asked Lakshmana.

"If you stop me during my talk, I'll go astray and then everything will go upset. Whatever questions arise in your mind while listening to me, you string them together in one knot. After one answer is over, you can untie the bundle of questions." Lakshmana acted as if he were cross with him.

"It's all right. Now I won't open my mouth. Say further."

"How can I speak further? I don't know where I left the thread of my talk. It was you who broke in, now you yourself tell me what I was saying." Lakshmana reinforced his voice of supposed anger.

Guha began to scratch his head when he couldn't think out what to say.

"What was the need for you to interrupt me when you can't remember what I was saying?"

"Yes, now I remember. You were saying that Shri Rama put forward many reasons expressing his inability to take Sita Ma with him." It seemed that Guha paid no heed to Lakshmana's sarcasm.

"Yes!" Lakshmana felt happy when he got the hint where he had left his talk. He proceeded to say further in the same style, "But Sita Mata refused to carry out Shri Rama's command related to any apprehension and greed. In one sentence itself did she disarm Shri Rama."

"Which sentence?" Guha opened his mouth to ask.

"I knew you'd interrupt me"

"I…I…me," Guha became hesitant.

"Don't worry because I know that it's your curiosity connected with the context of my talk. It proves that the listener is alert and awake; he hasn't gone to sleep," Lakshmana tried to efface the marks of shamefulness on the face of Guha. "She said: without her, Rama is incomplete. After marriage, a man without his spouse is incomplete. So, if he goes to the forest all alone, it would mean that he would fulfill his half promise. Simultaneously, she showed the terrific face of a wife to Shri Rama." Lakshmana laughed, "Was that her divine weapon? But I'm not going to narrate that to you. It was the personal talk between the two spouses."

"What were the obstacles before you, tell me that," Guha also laughed.

"First is that Urmila should permit me to go cheerily and second is that Mother Sumitra should also do the same." Lakshmana continued to speak with the same flow, "Urmila told me that the first chapter of princesses' learning was to bury into oblivion one's personal comforts at the time of adversity and find out the means to protect the country." She said: I am first a princess, and then a wife. If we lead a more comfortable and more luxurious life than our subject, we must be prepared to make more sacrifices than they do when time demands.

Our responsibilities are many times more than those of the common people. Our personal life is only accidental. The duty of a royal person is to look after the welfare of the people. I observed that mother gave you permission with a great sense of pride. What a magnanimous heart she has! Not a spark of doubt arose in her mind." Lakshmana said, " Do you know, Nishadraja! what my mother said to me? She said that I was fortunate enough to get a golden opportunity of serving Shri Rama. She exhorted me to seek the image of my father in Rama, hers in Sita and Ayodhya in the forest."

"Now I understand the deep implication of addressing Sitaji as "Sita Mata!" A streak of astonishment conjured up on Guha's brow, "Shri Rama is like your father, I understand this; but what does it mean that the forest is like Ayodhya?"

Lakshmana felt as if astounded. He repeated this sentence many a time as if he were in prayer. But he didn't try to understand its implication hidden in the last message. "What are you thinking?" intervened Guha.

"That you have said a wonderful thing, friend! It's really true that we go on repeating words without musing. Those words also lose their efficacy if we don't probe the secrecy behind them. Never did I attempt to know the implication of looking upon the forest as Ayodhya. There's definitely some hidden meaning of it. Never have I conjectured about it. I took it to be an ordinary sentence said in an ordinary way."

"Your mother is extraordinary. Whatever she says will have its deep meaning. You'll have to decode it, Lakshamana."

"What you say has some weight," said Lakshmana, musing over that sentence.

"Look here, Prince Lakshmana!" Guha spoke. "This time you're dead tired. Shri Rama is bound by his promise, but not you. Have a taste of delicacies brought by me for you and enjoy the sleep on a soft bed peacefully. Then you can cudgel your brain to discover the meaning of this sentence. I am here for the protection of Shri Rama. The troubles of forests are for us. We're the dwellers of forests by temperament.

Nothing of the forest is hidden from us. I'll stay awake for you."

"I honour your sentiments, faultless Nishadraja! But if I try to draw out the meaning of this last sentence, I'll rely upon my imagined intelligence. It may be that the meaning I discover doesn't even touch the spirit behind this sentence. Then I'll ask God-like Shri Rama to give me its definite meaning." Lakshmana didn't let Guha speak about it any more. "It's your attitude imbued with duty consciousness and your sense of affiliation with us that you're so careful and alert about rendering your service to us and safeguarding us. But tell me one thing how I can get buried in a sleep on a beautiful and soft bed brought for me when Shri Rama, all-potent, is sleeping on a straw-woven mat on the earth. When my adored Shri Rama has been content for two nights with drinking only water, it's unimaginable for me even to think of taking palatable food just to keep my body and soul together. I'm frequented by only one question whether our parents will remain alive till the completion of the period of exile. Shall we be able to enter Ayodhyapuri after completing the long period of banishment? After all, we'll have to go back to Ayodhya after fulfilling our promise of fourteen years of exile. The most thirsty and discontented eyes are awaiting us there. Moreover, we have given them word that we shall return to Ayodhya. May the Supreme Infinite Being keep showering His blessings upon us!" Looking at Shri Rama and Sita who were sleeping with contentment writ on their faces, Lakshmana greeted them reverentially by bowing his head.

TWO

"Where's Urmila?" Sumitra asked the chief-maid.

"After her bath and prayer, the princess went to the library. She said that it would be her daily routine. She would spend most of her time only in meditation and studies. She would try to remain silent quite often for fourteen years. She would converse only with you. If other mothers asked her anything, she would simply answer their questions. She would not join in any family festival, social function, religious or political organisations. Except you, she would not discharge any social obligation towards anyone else."

With a gesture of her hand, Sumitra told her to be silent.

The maid-servant obeyed her.

"Did the princess eat anything?"

“Yes, your Ladyship!”

“What?”

“Fruits.”

“Sumitra thought for a moment and then asked the chief-maid, “What did Urmila take for her dinner at night?’

“The coarse food that came from ashrams of forest dwellers.”

“And what sorts of fruit-items today?”

“Your Ladyship! Root vegetables from the forest.”

“And you fetched all these things for her!” There was a touch of pain in Sumitra’s voice, “Your duty is to serve her with nutritious and balanced diet, and not to arrange forest food and fruits for her. Every fruit from the palace is first tested by food experts and then it is sent to the kitchen. And you - you sent the princess forest food and fruits! If by mistake any poisonous forest fruit came! Have you forgotten your duties?”

“If Your Ladyship permits me to stay fearless,

I want to say something with humility," the chief-maid folded her hands and bowed her head.

"Speak out!" Sumitra thought that the maid was going to cover up her mistake by giving her some formal reason. She wanted to go to Urmila soon after listening to her supplication.

"I know what my duties are. I've been kept in service to fulfill every desire of the princess. It's only after getting them tested I sent forest food and fruits to her." The chief-maid looked towards Sumitra and spoke in her gentle, meek voice, "If I hadn't fulfilled the wishes of the princess, I could have been asked why I failed to get her available all that she wanted."

"You could inform me about it." It appeared that Sumitra was somewhat appeased with the chief-maid's plea.

"I thought it would be unreasonable."

"It appeared to be unreasonable." Whatever contentment Sumitra had in her mind burst out suddenly in the form of dissatisfaction. "What was unreasonable in it?"

SHASHI

"In that case you could have given your first command not to get forest food and fruit and then you could proceed to meet the princess at once so as to know the reason of her desiring so."

"Yes, this is what could have happened. But what's wrong in it?" After hearing the chief-maid, Sumitra felt vexed.

"It would have been the starting-point of unfairness, Your Ladyship!" The chief-maid bent her head, "This context could have sent a message to her that I was your secret agent, a spy, serving as a personal attendant of hers and that I had been appointed to keep an eye upon her."

Sumitra kept looking fascinatingly at the chief-maid. Her discretion had checked a wrong message from going to Urmila who could have interpreted such a delicate matter in any other sense.

"I am quite happy with your sense of understanding." Sumitra's voice had a touch of softness. "I am proud of you."

"May Your Ladyship keep upon me your kindly looks." The chief-maid bowed her head. Sumitra's foot-steps moved towards the library. Motivated by Rama, Lakshmana had got this library built. Rama had at his disposal not only a grand library but also a group of many erudite persons. They gave him information about the spiritual origins discovered by many types of ascetics. Lakshmana had a store displaying many arms and weapons which outbeat each other. He used to worship his weapons day in and day out. One day Sumitra saw him carrying a treasure of books in a separate chariot. When she asked him what it was all, he told her excitedly that Rama had exhorted him that the knowledge of mere weapons went to boost up one's vanity. He had further advised him that a Kshatriya should respect not only weapons but also Shastras (scriptures); that it was only a Shastra which told them the real aim of equipping oneself with arms and weapons and also when and to what extent they should be used. Weapons minus Shastras were like a speedy chariot minus reins. After this, Lakshmana started studying

Shastras. Quite often did Rama send a book to him to study and then he would adorn the library with it like a precious stone.

Sumitra placed her hand on the back of Urmila who was sitting in Lakshmana's library, quite engrossed in her studies.

"Oh, Mother, you!" Urmila got aghast, shut her book and touched Sumitra's feet.

"Did you think that it was Lakshmana!" said Sumitra in order to ease the gravity of the situation. But, soon after this, she realised her mistake that she shouldn't have said so. It was like sprinkling salt over one's wounds.

"It's only a matter of fourteen years. He'll again startle me as in the past he did." There was a streak of anguish in Urmila's smile.

"Daughter! I don't know how I should reduce your pain. At present, except for certain merciless people, all others are distressed caused by Shri Rama's banishment. But your distress!"

"I've sought solace even from this unusual suffering. God wants to keep me away from my lord for a long duration. He has been kind enough to choose a fourteen-year test for me instead of separating us forever. Time is powerful, Mother! I'm thinking of filling the void of that portion of time with meditation," spoke Urmila.

"Urmi! Is it, I think, your way of expressing your mental protest?"

"I want to utilise this time for my spiritual development, and not for nurturing my vices. You had blessed him saying that he should live in the forest as if he were in Ayodhya. Bless me also that I live in Ayodhya as if I were in the forest."

"Daughter!" Sumitra's eyes were filled with tears. She made Urmila cling to her breast and said, "This is not a blessing, but a curse."

"If poison is used with dexterity, it results in divine nectar and if the nectar is used unjudiciously, its results are venomous."

"If you set your heart upon amusement, you won't know how days passed." Sumitra tried to make her understand, "This kind of solitary life will be like a prison-house."

"To set one's heart on leading an epicurean life will be an illusion. It'll be like a person who starts consuming alcoholic drinks to forget his sufferings. The effect of pleasures and luxuries of life is more fatal than that of drinking. You yourself tell me if it will behove a woman, whose sinless husband is leading an austere life of a recluse, to lead a luxurious life."

"I want to spend this duration of time by keeping myself awake, and not by letting myself go to sleep. I've dedicated this time to my inner journey. I firmly believe that you'll keep away from me all the obstacles that come in my way and make my solitariness beautiful and successful."

"Amen!" Sumitra placed her hand on Urmila's head and blessed her.

"How're you bearing your sufferings?" asked Urmila.

Sumitra kept on looking at her with pride: what a vast difference between Shrutakirti and Urmila! And Shatrughana and Lakshmana! Till today she took Urmila to be an ordinary daughter-in-law. 'Ordinary' means a daughter-in-law well versed in all civilities of life. She is overbrimmed with love for both of her daughters-in-law. She looks after both of them as if they were small children and she keeps her affectionate looks upon them. But at this odd time she is respectful to Urmila who is filled with divinity. She is feeling that in respect of self-power and spiritual journey she is less developed than Urmila. Nobody has asked her how she is bearing her pain. Whosoever she comes across, she says that it's a matter of sorrow that Lakshmana too is accursed. Or someone says that a mother should be like Sumitra to whet her vanity. But she knows that all these are hollow words, and not heart-felt words. It's only a formal social statement. On the other hand, there's Shrutakirti - like princesses of simple and common disposition. She finds no fault in her. There's no fault of any kind in her. But she doesn't have the profundity of Urmila's heart. Up till now, she looked upon Shrutakirti and Urmila through the eyes of a mother-in-law-cum-guardian. But now she can't see Urmila from this perspective. Now she regards Urmila as her guru and she, her disciple. She has to know and learn many things from Urmila.

“Many questions related to the mysteries of life often arise in me. If occasionally I meet some able person, I discuss those things with him or her. I didn’t know that there was a worthy person in the house itself. I’d wish my questions to be the greatest obstacle in the path of your solitariness. Will it pose any inconvenience to you?” Sumitra asked lovingly.

“Good fortune can never be an inconvenient thing. But it’s not true that I’m a worthy and able person,” spoke Urmila.

“It’s my view-point. There’s no reflection of any woman in the Ganga, even then the world calls her ‘Mother’. The world says that Lakshmana is under obligation to lead an austere life which is nothing but a punishment for him. What does it mean? Is banishment not a punishment for Rama? Is it not so for Sita? Is this marriage not a punishment for you? Is it not an occasion of distress for me?” Sumitra unlocked her heart, “At least I don’t understand this riddle.”

"This is the very quality of mystery that it's beyond our understanding. No inauguration of mystery is possible. So far as punishment is concerned, it's all concerted, combined. When a huge wave is caused to rise by someone, it leaves its impact upon the farthest shores. It's the speciality of waves that they first form circles and then spread. Our surging is the outcome of that huge wave. Whatever name we give to it, it depends on our dictionary of language and nothing can be said immediately about the result of any wave. It's just like a fruit-bearing plant. Until it grows into a full-fledged tree, nothing can definitely be announced about what type of fruit it would bear."

"But if we plant a mango tree, it will bear only mangoes," spoke Sumitra.

"But it can't be declared who will be the consumers of those mangoes, whether it will be healthy mangoes or not and how many mangoes it will bear. This is all uncertain. In Ayodhya this family feud has revolutionized its politics. The incident is related to the family and its impact is on its politics. That's why I said that everything here is inter-connected."

"You asked me how I was bearing my sufferings. Now I ask you to tell me how I should bear my sufferings," Sumitra's voice was overbrimmed with sadness.

"In the same way as you have been doing up till now. This is a beautiful way of bearing one's sufferings." There was respect for Sumitra in Urmila's eyes.

"How I'm bearing my pain, I don't know." Sumitra was amazed to note how Urmila had introspected her fully.

"Since you help all others to bear sufferings, it's giving you strength to bear your sufferings. In this tempest, you're like that important sail of the royal ship of Ayodhya which is giving its impetus to the ship."

"Which of the two - Kekai and Maharaja Dashratha, is more guilty?" asked Sumitra, paying no attention to Urmila's compliments.

"The language of the question is pregnant with presumptions and conclusions. So the language of the neutral questioner is to be moulded first. It's very necessary," spoke Urmila.

"Your question assumes that both of them are really at fault. Only the extent of their guilt is to be fixed. But the language of a healthy question should be whether either of the two - Kekai and Maharaja Dashratha - is guilty or not."

"Taking it to be a question of mine, answer it," said Sumitra.

"To express his gratitude and his eternal joy, the Maharaja, in my view, had given his word. Now to prove it true, all the associates of Maharaja are paying its price in their own way. Shri Rama is paying the price of his filial allegiance to his father. Lakshmana, the price of his fraternal love; Sita and I, for being the spouses, and the Maharaja is paying the price of his paternal love. Some are sucking pleasures out of it. Some, the feeling of pride and some are feeling distressed. But somehow or the other, the price is being paid. If Shri Rama had disregarded these vows, the price might have chosen its path to get itself paid."

"What could have been the eventuality?"

"We are still ignorant about the road speed. Who knows what is hidden in the closed palm of time? It will be known only when it opens," spoke Urmila.

"I'm worried to think what shape the incidents will take on Bharata's return. How will Bharata behave with Shatrughana? How will he feel that the brother of that Shatrughana with whom he had cordial relations had accompanied his step-brother out of love for fourteen years of exile, and he himself is sitting on the royal throne in place of that brother? Will he be able to make Shatrughana his confidant or will Shatrughana himself be able to call Bharata's coronation just and appropriate? What will happen if Shatrughana insists on going to the forest after Shri Rama and Lakshmana? May be that one brother becomes the enemy of another?" Sumitra felt relieved after opening her heart to Urmila. Who else was there before whom she could unfold her heart? This time everyone was busy expressing his or her griefs in a magnified manner. It was only Urmila who was afflicted with genuine grief. She was the one who could never leak out what transpired between them.

Kissing the hands of Sumitra, Urmila said, "What lies in your hand or in my hand or in anybody else's hand? The time is out of joint. It is casting its shadow like black clouds. Somewhere there may be a flash of lightning. Somewhere water may shoot out of the earth and somewhere there may be hailstorm. Somewhere there may be torrential rainfall and somewhere snowfall. What can be said? You simply witness these events with a calm mind. Whatever happens will happen and we shall play our role, whatever be."

"Kekai's vengeance has terrified sister Kausalya." Without paying any heed to Urmila's statement, Sumitra expressed her worry, "She (Kausalya) thinks that Kekai has been sitting still up till now. But as Bharata takes possession of the kingdom, she'll again exhibit her terrific visage. She won't leave any stone unturned in tormenting and doing harm to her. She will want to have the kingdom for Bharata without any thorns or stumbling block. She would like to remove Rama and all his associates taking them to be the thorns in the way of Ayodhya regime. Say something about it."

"I don't think that Bharata will join hands with his mother Kekai in this vicious pursuit. I'm of the view that Bharata has no knowledge of this whole episode." Urmila said, "If Bharata had his hands in this plot, he wouldn't have kept away from Ayodhya up till now. It may be that he didn't manifest his presence here at that time but he would have suddenly appeared here for his coronation soon after the departure of Shri Rama for the forest. Nobody wants any kind of delay in such cases when fructified. Secondly, no date was fixed in advance for coronation. The whole process was arranged suddenly. It was a sort of emergency. Many times I've heard talks of these brothers, saying that Bharata has no interest in kingly duties. He is only desirous of leading a carefree life of simple responsibilities. He says that there is no need for him to look after the administrative work of the kingdom as long as father, elder brother Rama and Lakshmana are there. He and Shatrughana get joy out of pleasure trips.

So I don't think that Bharata will align himself to his mother and look upon his relations as his enemies and retaliate upon them.

"It sounds good to me. But on what basis are you saying all this?"

"The same basis I've just told you; that is his dedication to Shri Rama."

Sumitra laughed. Urmila thought that perhaps she had said a stupid thing.

"Did I say any unharmonious thing? asked Urmila.

"What you said was not out of harmony, but circumstances have made it unharmonious."

"I don't understand you."

"It seems to you that Bharata who is devoted to Rama won't join hands with his mother and think of doing any harm to him. Did anyone of us ever think that Kekai who flaunted her love for Rama more than her son would indulge in such a fatal assault? So, I don't understand whom to trust." Sumitra wiped the drops of perspiration on her forehead.

"I beg your pardon, Mother! But such a statement whom to trust and whom not is in itself childish. All should be trusted till the time the trust is not breached or assassinated. If one person breaches the trust, we can't hold the entire totality responsible for it. Nor does one person represent the temperament of all men of the world. If it had been so, all the sons of the world should have been dedicated to their father like Shri Rama. If anyone proves to be a disobedient son, the world then will say that it is meaningless to long for a son. It seems that people have lost their faith in their sons. But on seeing a son like Shri Rama, nobody has made any such a statement that sons have made themselves worthy of pride. Nobody will now be able to charge the sons with disobedience. Shri Rama has blotted out the stigma on all disobedient sons. Could it ever be thought that any brother would feel pleased by sacrificing himself and his spouse's life for the sake of his step-brother? Why do we allow treacherous acts to enshrine themselves in the temple of our heart? And we don't happen to see the value of sacrifices! We always welcome the negative feelings from the core of our heart and conveniently forget the positive feelings, taking them to be our mental illusions. If any part of our body suffers from any kind of ailment, we get assured of its pain and get it cured. But if any wave of divinity touches us and gives us joy while in meditation, we're over-brimmed with doubt and suspicion. We owe our distrust to our thinking whether it was true or only our mental figment. We never entertain any disbelief in our physical and mental pain thinking that whatever we're feeling as inauspicious may be simply our doubt. Tell me whether you expected any such unique deed from your son, Lakshmana. If he himself had not been so excited for exile, would you have permitted your son to accompany Shri Rama to go to the forest? Tell me this."

"No, I'd never expected such a kind of sacrifice on the part of Lakshmana. Nor did anyone else. This world can't expect such a kind of sacrifice from any brother. And it's also true that if Lakshmana himself hadn't told me about his going along with Rama for exile, it wouldn't have occurred to me that he should accompany him. When I saw that Lakshmana was determined to go, I didn't want to be an obstacle in his way. At that time I left you alone with him because you're his wife. You will never want that your husband should keep away from you. I hoped that you'd prevent him from going in the name of your claim upon him as his better-half."

"He informed me that Shri Rama wouldn't agree to take him with him if I didn't give him my assent happily. He assured me that if I didn't give him my consent, he wouldn't go."

"And you gave him your assent gladly?" bewildered Sumitra looked at Urmila. Her looks were scolding her for what she'd done. Why did she repeat the mistake which she herself had committed? Sumitra tried to probe her heart: She remembers that when Lakshmana came to tell her that he was resolute to accompany Shri Rama to go to the forest, she had felt deeply hurt and wounded. In a niche of her mind she had thought what was the need for him to go to the forest with Rama. Why should he undergo the punishment given to Rama by father? And to go to the forest with Rama means to consign his whole life to the flames of fire - the fire to which he was not invited. It's like burning oneself in the fire without any rhyme or reason. Then the same heart had prodded her to say that he wouldn't be given permission to go to the forest. It was perhaps her maternal love-lorn heart. In such a case, she wouldn't have probably refrained him from going to the forest, but it would have reduced his respect for her in his heart - not only reduced but destroyed it in toto. It's because Lakshmana is always in favour of destroying everything. It's the infinite grace of God upon her that she didn't listen to the voice of her love-ridden heart, otherwise her state would also have been like that of Kekai whose love-ridden heart got the things done, the result of which the whole world is witnessing and suffering from. She discovered that if she was able to hear the voice of her conscience more clearly, it was because of the blessings of the luminous souls. Just then she felt that Urmila had understood the love-lorn feelings of her heart. Not to let her know her hesitance any more, she asked Urmila, "Why did you do so? Why didn't you prevent Lakshmana from going to the forest? You're his better-half. It would have seemed more convenient and more natural if you'd checked him?"

"It means that you didn't want him to go to the forest?" Urmila stared at her with her probing eyes.

Sumitra couldn't bear the brunt of her looks. She shrank from within to realise that Urmila had read all her feelings very well - the ones that she had up till now kept hidden from her. Now if she attempted to conceal her ill-thoughts from her, it would be tantamount to hiding one's ailment from a physician.

"Probably it was my maternal love-ridden heart," said Sumitra. "I wanted to save my son from the rigours of banishment on the grounds of maternal love. But what thought of yours didn't let you prevent Lakshmana from going?"

"It didn't mean that I took no step in this

regard. I'd a revolting attitude towards this behaviour of his."

"Then what was its outcome?"

"The same as it happened to your motherly love. I felt almost gulled when I saw his devotion and dedication to Shri Rama. His sentiments for his brother were so intense that my selfish moto couldn't stay before it. Nor did I contribute to it in anyway. Didn't he desire to spend the precious time of his youth with his spouse? Who doesn't do so? But he'd transformed his lustful energy into love-energy. I thought it would be scandalous on my part to pull him down from a high pedestal of life to the low pedestal of mire again. I didn't want that valiant Lakshmana should kill his spirit and live the life of an animal tied to a hunter's place, feeling degraded and low in his own eyes." There was some vivacity in Urmila's voice.

"Why, could he have been enslaved in Ayodhya?" There was a chink of trouble in Sumitra's voice.

"He had told me that if I didn't give him my assent, he would not go back to show his face to Shri Rama and would never be able to forgive himself throughout his life. The separation from a proud and valiant husband is better than the company of a self-condemned husband." Urmila's eyes turned red on account of the feeling of valour, and watery because of excessive love.

A heart-rending cry arose in her. Oh! She is the one who is a true female Kshatriya who sends her husband to the battle-field by putting up a streak of red powder on his brow with pride and cheerfulness. No dark thoughts and suspicion intruded upon her. She is fixed like northern star, determined, resolute and immovable.

"Daughter! If you really wanted to lead a rigorous and austere life like Lakshmana, you could also have embarked on that journey with him. At least Sita could have got a friend in you. And you also could have been with your lord." Sumitra passed her hand affectionately on Urmila's head.

"I had put this proposal before him. But if I had accompanied him, it would have divided his concentration on service. To discharge his responsibilities towards me could have distressed him. Then he would have to serve with divided thoughts whereas for a devotee, the unshaken devotion is better."

Sumitra felt that if she stayed with Urmila for some time more, she might place her head upon her feet out of respect. She would, no doubt, be benefited but Urmila wouldn't cherish it.

"Fine Daughter! I make a move. The physical health of Maharaja is deteriorating day by day. Looking after him and sister, I keep myself under control." Sumitra got up, "Before going, I want to say one thing to you. I feel gratified to get you as my daughter-in-law. May God bless you with success in your inner journey!"

After the departure of Sumitra, the chief-maid entered.

"Listen! Remove all the cosmetics and adornments from my chamber and keep them in the basement. If possible, only after fourteen years, they'll appear here. In the middle part of the palace there is a garden. Let there be a bamboo cottage and a mat interwoven with grass on the ground to sleep on. For food there should be only leaves and earthen pots. The food should not be better than the one which is easily available for forest dwellers. Unless and until I summon anyone, none should come and disturb me in my solitariness." There was strictness in Urmila's voice.

"It will be as you desire, My Ladyship!" The chief-maid bowed her head and said, "I've a curiosity."

"Say!"

"If anybody comes to meet you or if there's any message for you, will you, in that case, permit me to come to you?"

"Try your best not to contact me for any unwarranted message or visitor. Any message that comes for me should be sent to Mother Sumitra. She'll decide what's right for me. The upshot is that whosoever or whatsoever comes to me will have the consent of Mother Sumitra. The rest I leave to your discretion. You're free to take your decision in an emergency."

"It's necessary for me to come and go to see the arrangement of things in the chamber. May I have your consent to enter the building without your permission if there is any such need?"

"There's no restriction on your arrival and departure."

"May I continue to enjoy your Ladyship's graces!" The chief-maid bowed her head and slunk away.

* * *

Urmila closed her eyes with the image of Lakshmana in her mind. She took some long, deep breaths and then let her body loose. A sort of energy rose from her root chakra and went speedily to her crown chakra on finding all other channels closed. She felt that she was flying in the sky. She got penetrating eye-sight. She went on flying in the welkin. Flying over the animals grazing in villages and fields, forests and rivers that fell on the way, she reached mentally a gigantic and beautiful tree situated on a distant mound where Sita and Rama were sitting. She visualised that Lakshmana had brought forest food for them. He's planning to make a cottage for them but Shri Rama was telling him that

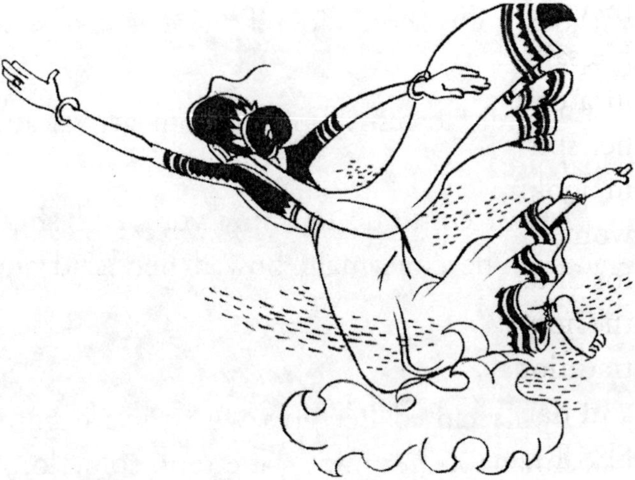

SHASHI

they were not yet giving a halt to their journey. He said that that place where they would stay in a cottage hadn't yet come. She also saw on her spiritual plane that Sumantra was engaged in looking after the horses, and many tribal women had brought different kinds of flowers for Sita. Sita had accepted them all happily. In the honour of Sita, they were playing upon their traditional musical instruments, singing folklores and dancing. Some tribal men were sitting by Shri Rama. He was discussing something with them. Lakshmana was engrossed in listening to the discussion. Urmila descended from the sky and silently sat by Sita. She was glad that she was invisible to them but she was witnessing and listening to everything.

THREE

On the banks of the Ganga the dawn was the most beautiful of all times. The gentle wind was sporting with the ripples of the Ganga and they were producing the sweet murmuring sound like a running child endowed with energy who plays with the heifers of cows and feels amused. The cuckoos were practicing like a classical singer. The forest area was resounding with peacocks' scream. It seemed as if the sweet-scented breeze and the leaves falling from the tree like a waterfall had built a dream-world. The flock of leaping deer peeping from behind the trees was amazed to see who had taken possession of their mound. The birds, while flying, were warbling folklores in the sky.

Before the early dawn, Rama took a dip in the Ganga and sat in meditation. His face was replete with calm contentment. In his wet, disentangled, long black hair, he looked as if he were a living Shiva in meditation.

SHASHI

Guha along with his counsellors was discussing something with Lakshmana. Many women from Guha's family had brought baskets full of garlands for Sita. The beauty of fragrant flowers was wonderful and looked different from the ones growing in the palace garden. These flowers were really craziest in sweat smell. The women began to sing tribal songs. Along with dance, the clinking sound of ornaments was touching the soul. Though Sita didn't understand the language of their songs yet their sweet sound was hypnotizing Sita.

When Rama's meditation was over, he stood up with bark cloth on his shoulder. He bowed his head before the Sun-god rising in the east. He passed his palms on his face as if the Sun-god were an earthen lamp in the sky and he was taking blessings from it.

All advanced towards Rama when they saw that his meditation was over. Lakshmana placed a basketful of ripe, sweet-smelling fruits before Rama.

"Will I eat all this all alone?" laughed Rama.

"You haven't eaten anything for a long time. So Lakshmana wants you to eat and compensate the loss of many past days," laughed Guha also.

"Compensation for the loss or complete loss!" One of the counsellors of Guha twirled the end of his moustache and said, "O Lord! Kindly eat as much as you like and leave for us the remaining used ones."

"Do you think friends and brethren come for eating the used ones?" Rama reached for the basket and whatever fruit came in his hand was shared with Guha and his present counsellors. He peeled off the skin of a banana and said, "We'll all together eat it. The Vedas say that the person who eats alone and doesn't share it with others is a sinner."

"I never ate such a sweet guava in my whole life." Lakshmana said, "These fruits are very succulent. If we eat them, we'll feel neither hungry nor thirsty even after walking a long distance for one full duration of time."

"Nature had made them mellow and juicy, Lakshmana!" Guha said, "Nature has ripened

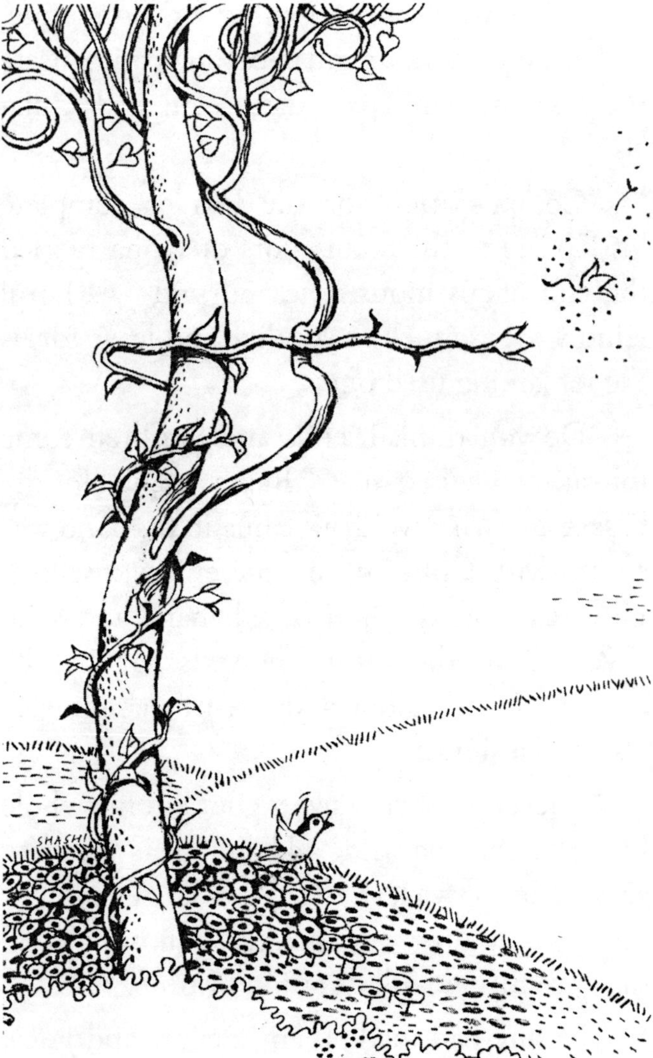
SHASHI

them on trees. In Ayodhya, fruit traders sell stale fruits of many days. Stale fruits are as tasteless as the stale food."

"O Lord! Shringverpur owes its gratitude to you at present. We hope that you'll spend the rest period of your exile here itself," an old counsellor of Guha prayed to Rama with his folded hands.

Rama smiled and looked at Lakshmana.

"It's Shri Rama's wish that we should cross the Ganga as the day dawns and enter the desolate forest. This is such a place as anyone can come here easily and then our banishment will turn into city-dwelling." A laughter floated on Lakshmana's face. "The people of adjoining districts will think that there is Shri Rama Fair in Shringverpur and so they'll bring their merchandise and set up their stalls to sell their goods. This place will be known as 'Neo Ayodhyapuri' instead of 'Shringverpur'."

All those present there laughed in such a way as if they would burst into tears.

"We want a boat to go across the Ganga.

It's hoped that Nishadraja Guha won't pray to Shri Rama for lingering his stay here but will fulfill his wish at once." Lakshmana smiled and looked at Guha.

Guha felt as if someone had robbed him of his riches and he had become a pauper. He looked at his counsellors with a sad heart and said, "The most beautiful and grandest boat on the ghat belongs to a boatman, Kevat. Tell him to be prepared and bring the boat to our exclusive ghat. We're all coming there."

"Not exclusive but the ordinary ghat for common people. We'll board the boat from the place meant for common masses. Arrange for our necessary things to be brought into the boat," intervened Rama.

"Carry out every word of Shri Rama's orders as it is," said Guha, looking at his counsellors.

The counsellors went away to arrange for the boat.

"And what else is to be carried out, Lord!" Guha folded his hands.

"The word 'order' is not appropriate.

Honouring your feelings, Shri Rama has expressed his desire before you lest you should think that you didn't get any chance of serving him," laughed Lakshmana and saved the whole atmosphere from being surged with emotions.

"Friend!" Rama said to Guha, "Arrange for the extract of a banyan tree for us. I've heard that the ascetics apply it to their hair so that they may have entwined strands of hair. Our austere life in Shringverpur will get this make-up."

Rama and Lakshmana equipped themselves with armour over their bark clothes. They suspended a sword on one side and loaded their backs with a quiver of arrows and a bow in their hands. Sita also came there when she saw them ready to go. When the women from the Guha's family saw Sita ready to go, they started wailing. Sita tried her best to console them, but the more she tried to give themselves solace, the more they wept bitterly.

Sumantra drove the chariot to go to the bathing steps. Rama, Lakshmana and Sita occupied their seats in the chariot.

"We will accompany you upto the bathing-steps on our horses," said Guha.

Lakshmana stretched his hands towards Guha and said, "Don't be so much cross, friend! Come, ascend the chariot with us."

Guha also extended his hand. The charioteer started driving. The bewailing women were singing songs. They were running after the chariot, showering upon them their flowers. Their young children were also running with them. They couldn't understand what so happened that their mothers who were up till now were happily singing and dancing started weeping and singing sad songs all of a sudden. The chariot stopped when it reached the common bathing-ghat. There was a huge boat at the ghat. It was adorned with multi-coloured flags. Just then Guha's servant came with a pitcher which was full of the milk extracted from a banyan tree.

"Come, Lakshmana! Sit here for some time and entwine your hair. There are no means and no facility for hair style in the forests." Rama turned towards Sumantra. Touching him with his right hand, he said, "Kaka! I've travelled in the chariot up to this place by the order of the Maharaja. Now we've to travel further into desolate, lonely forests. So you should return to the Maharaja soon and live there quite carefully."

"Shri Rama!" Sumantra was afflicted with grief and began to weep.

Lakshmana whispered something into Guha's ears, and Guha into his secretary's. All the secretaries of Guha with their soldiers made a circle, keeping sufficiently away from Shri Rama, and sat silently with their bent heads.

"We are undone by the hands of destiny in every way." Sumantra burst into tears, "That destiny hasn't spared even you. It means that celibacy, study of the Vedas, simplicity, sacredness, kindness, etc are all futile virtues. What will happen to the sinful persons like us when destiny shows no mercy even to the virtuous persons? On the one hand, we're deprived of your visits and, on the other hand, there's no end of the sufferings of the natives of Ayodhya because of the vicious Kekai.

O Lord! Though my language for the lord should be reverential yet you should pardon me since I'm your devotee if I happen to use harsh words audaciously. I'm only praying to ask you how I'll return to Ayodhya with this face of mine when the kingdom is plunged in deep sorrow because of the son's affliction. The entire Ayodhya will call me a sinner who has taken Rama to the forest. I won't be able to show my face to anyone. The whole Ayodhya is a witness to what I've done. When they see me return to Ayodhya with the chariot without you, their condition will be like of the ones who see the charioteer in the chariot without the warrior who has sacrificed his life in the war. You yourself have witnessed how at the time of your departure, the people had made an outcry. When they see the chariot empty, their bewailing will magnify a hundred times more. And these horses of mine were accustomed to carrying your friends and relatives happily. They'll not be able to pull the empty chariot out of sorrow. When the Maharani, Kausalya asks me about you, I'll not be able to tell her a

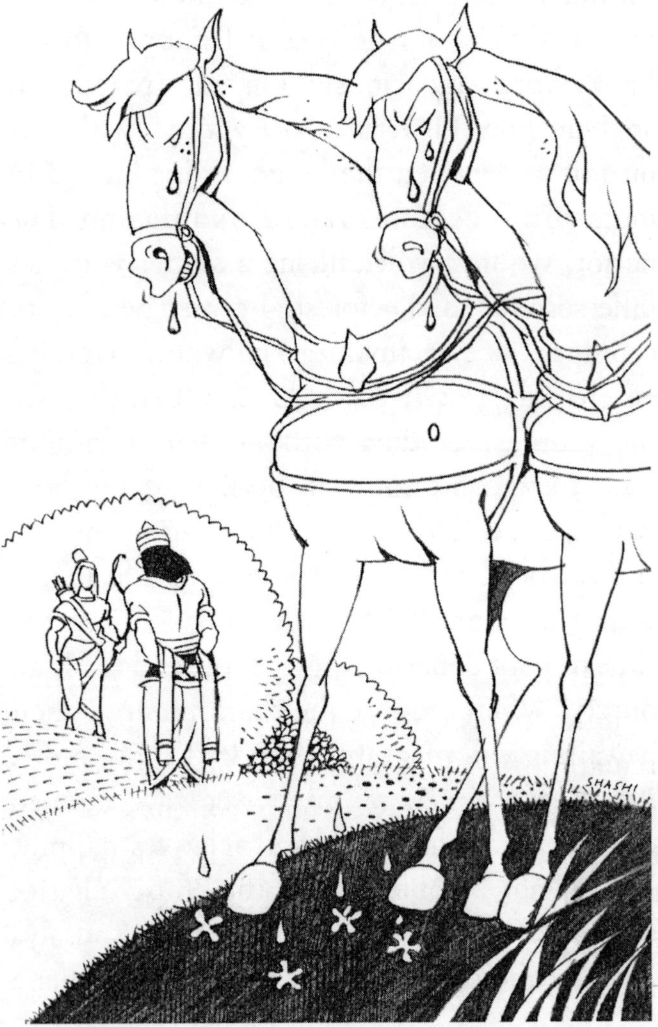
SHASHI

lie that I've taken you to your maternal uncle's house and so she should feel assured. Neither will I be able to tell that lie nor speak the truth that I've left you in a dense forest. Then how can I return to Ayodhya? I'll also accompany you for banishment and if I remained alive, I would return to Ayodhya with you in the same chariot, otherwise I would leave my mortal coil while serving you. If you didn't permit me to accompany you, I would get into the fire with this chariot."

Like a naughty child, Lakshmana entertained a thought in his mind that he should tell Kaka to return the best horses of the Maharaja to Nishadraja Guha before entering the fire with the chariot. It would be good if he consigned himself to fire. It would liberate his family from the duty of performing the last rite of his cremation and the kingdom would also give full economic assistance to his family on the grounds that he lost his life while discharging his official duty. But it seemed that Shri Rama enthroned in Lakshmana's heart showed his severe eyes to Lakshmana and told him to remain within his bounds because every time one can't indulge in fun and frolic.

"I make your hair by applying this extracted natural and fragrant milk to your strands of hair so as to transform them into entwined hair. Till then you continue to listen to Kaka's talk." There was an echo of comical naughtiness in Lakshmana's voice. He took Rama's hair in his hands and looked at Guha for help.

"You are fit only for archery. This work is beyond your powers." Guha murmured, "Be assured. After Shri Rama's hair, I'll make your hair-style also."

Rama kept looking at Sumantra.

"You're my lord's son. It's my pious duty to serve you. I can't live in that cruel Ayodhya which is full of vicious machinations. As long as you were there, Ayodhya was a holy place. But now what is there for me to live for?" Sumantra now looked at Rama to see his reaction. It seemed that he had got tired of saying anything more now.

"Sumantraji!" Rama addressed him formally,

"Service to the lord is above all things as long as the lord is alive. The service to his son is implied in his service. The essence of religion hasn't vanished from Ayodhya. If we ourselves say such things, it'll leave a bad impact upon the common masses. At present, Ayodhya is passing through the ordeals of life. We're all wrestling with the challenges of our duties." Rama cast his meaningful looks upon Sumantra. When he spoke, there was a slight severity tinged with softness in his voice, "You say that there is nothing in Ayodhya for which one should live there! There is everything there. Maharaja Dashratha who is an embodiment of truth and religion lives there. He is the one who has not only made you the minister of his kingdom but also his close friend and has looked upon you as a dignified member of his family. And you say what is there in Ayodhya! The Maharaja hasn't trusted anybody else so much as you. That's why he chose you to see us off at such a long distance. It was you who were sent for me in an emergency. Like the most revered sage Narada, you enjoy the full liberty of coming and going anywhere in Ayodhya and at any time. The Maharaja has invested you with honour and privileges equal to his status. The same Maharaja Dashratha is now in Ayodhya. He is afflicted with old age and stricken with grief. Who else can dare go to him when he is in such a deplorable state. He keeps everyone else at a safe distance. You're the only one who can afford to be somewhat harsh in making him understand things if there is any such need. You're the only person who can give him solace and peace. There was nobody else in Ayodhya except you, Guru Vashishtha and the aged chief minister Siddhartha who could use harsh words in front of the Maharaja for his beloved queen Kekai. All were silent on account of fear and greed. All know that if they say anything against Kekai, they'll not only lose their job but may also possibly live the rest of their life in the dark cell. But you three spoke. All of you love the Maharaja excessively without any fear and lust. You could, therefore, speak all this. You also know that nobody in Ayodhya has so much courage as even to think of doing any harm to anyone of you. You should be all devoted to the

Maharaja. If you leave the Maharaja in lurch in Ayodhya, it will amount to cowardice and ingratitude on your part. If I'm also going to the forest, it's only to extensify his fame. You're the only person in Ayodhya who can control the situation. There are some deeper things also for which I'm asking you to return to Ayodhya."

Rama touched with both of his hands the strands of his hair entwined by Lakshmana and Guha, and got assured. He touched Sumantra with his right hand as a gesture to come closer to him. Sumantra slipped closer to Rama. There was secrecy in Rama's voice, "Whatever reasons I have given to you are, no doubt, very important but there are some other reasons also which can't be overlooked. It is, therefore, obligatory for you to return to Ayodhya for some unavoidable reasons. You're our most trustworthy source. If you return to Ayodhya, without us, our mother Kekai will be assured that whatever Rama had said has been fulfilled. If you don't return, she will think that Maharaja Dashratha is a liar and under your guidance he has made all arrangements of our banishment at a convenient and safe place. I don't want any kind of suspicion in her mind and for that reason, she will make an assault upon my sensitive father with her sarcasm. Do all that keeps the Maharaja happy. Whatever he and mother Kekai orders you to do, you must accomplish them and feel proud of showing your allegiance to them. Conduct my special errand for everyone and read it out in front of the Maharaja and all my mothers. First of all, convey my greetings to my father, Arya Dashratha and tell him that neither I nor Sita nor Lakshmana is grief-stricken for the reason that they had to leave Ayodhya to go to the forest. That we feel like on a pleasant excursion now. After fourteen years we shall return to Ayodhya to serve you. Also tell him not to leave Ayodhya in a chaotic condition. He should immediately send for Bharata for his coronation so that the prevailing conditions come to normalcy. After this, you should convey my greetings to all my mothers sitting with him and tell them that we're all in a condition we're satisfied with. Convey my special message to Bharata when he comes. Tell him that he should be as respectful in his conduct to all mothers as he is to the Maharaja. He shouldn't make any kind of distinction between his mother and all other mothers. He should look upon them with respect which they deserve." Rama became silent for some time. Then he pressed Sumantra's right arm with his pious, lotus-like soft hand to convey his intimacy and warmth, and said, "It all depends on you what immediate steps you'll take to control the situation in Ayodhya. This is not the time for being emotional but to struggle with the challenges of one's duty. No war gives us time or permission to shed tears. It says only one thing and it is that one should be cautious and alert. But it doesn't mean that a man should become insensitive. We have to be sensitive towards the safety and responsibilities of ours. Never let Bharata feel that he is not being accepted as the King of Ayodhya. As his companion, you should give assurance to the common masses that we all honour the decision of the Maharaja. You should make all efforts for the development of Ayodhya in the direction of Bharata. When all discern that you're respectful to the Maharaja and crown Prince Bharata, nobody will nourish any feeling of enmity in his heart. I wish that when mother Kekai finds that you've returned to Ayodhya, she'll feel contented on seeing Bharata ruling over the well-guarded Ayodhya. At present, the security of Ayodhya is of utmost importance in my eyes. If at such a critical time any invader casts his evil looks upon Ayodhya, it will be precarious for all. The safety of the kingdom is an essentiality. It makes no difference that I was not crowned as king. May Ayodhya be safe and prosperous! This is my ardent wish."

"If it's your order, I accept it with humility. Whatever you've said shall be done." Sumantra bowed his head.

"Nishadraja Guha!" Rama looked toward Guha, "I advised you also to be careful and alert about the safety and orderly state of your kingdom. All kings are quite often engrossed in their recreation and amusement. They simply make a show off that they are working for the welfare of the people. They impose a tax on the people for some reason or the other in order to collect money for their own comfort and luxuries. If a king has at his disposal the money collected from people, he shouldn't spend it on his comforts. That money is the legacy of the common masses and it should be utilised for their welfare. It is the duty of the king to see that the money which is given to the officials is used for the good of the people. There are many kings who shirk their work by saying that a king all alone can't do everything. But this is a way of either saving themselves or making inroads into corruption. One God all alone is looking after so many worlds and universe and He himself remains invisible. In the same way, a king is said to be God's representative. He can at least look after his kingdom in an appropriate manner.'

"Arya Rama!" spoke Sumantra.

"Say, Sumantraji!"

"As long as you were in Ayodhya, corruption was only in a capsule form, only in name. It's said that nature never destroys anything from its root. In the same way, corruption also has almost vanished from Ayodhya like a real creature. When you're not there, there is no fear of you. Without you how will crown prince Bharata be able to keep Ayodhya safe from this corruption? Now the seed of corruption will sprout like the wild grass and eat away the crop of good conduct of Ayodhya in the twinkling of an eye. The natives of Ayodhya had begun to call this epoch 'Ram-Rajya.' Ram-Rajya has become a synonym of beautiful, well-ordered and well-organised public administration. It seems that this 'Ram-Rajya' will become only a myth."

"No, nothing of this sort will occur. If any king has a skilled, worthy person like you, nothing of this kind can ever happen." Rama smiled, "You should again remind Bharata that there is only one effective way of ending corruption, and it is that one should make a sudden visit to any department anywhere in order to make an appraisal of the prevailing situation. As far as possible, one should be active among the people. The common run of people should feel secured. They should feel that the administration is keeping in mind their weal and woe. All this can be possible only when the officials have a fear in their mind that if they don't discharge their duties properly or if they indulge in any act of corruption, they can't escape from the eyes of the ruler. Whichever king does so, he rules not only on the earth but also on the hearts of people. The king should not take any undue advantage of the people's helplessness but conquer their hearts. The king should be such as is adored like God by the public. God is kind to the poor and the needy. He helps every helpless person. He doesn't take into consideration anybody's caste, faith, colour, face or riches while helping. He is like this sacred Mother Ganga that purges the vicious people. There is enough holy water for a thirsty person to quench his thirst with. Just as the Ganga is flowing with its cool water without making distinction of any kind, similarly, the king should also spend the riches kept in the treasury for a complete all-round development of the nation."

"My make-up is also over," attracting the attention of all, Lakshmana spoke.

"Lord! Seeing you both in these clothes,

nobody can call you princes. You're looking like some holy sage-sons". When Guha saw Rama and Lakshmana in their entwined hairstyle, he was overwhelmed with amazement.

"This is a good sign that we don't look like princes. It's good that we look ordinary persons," spoke Lakshmana in his own capricious style.

"Sumantraji! Whatever Lakshmana said to you, please don't convey it to the Maharaja as he'll feel hurt," Rama looked at Lakshmana smilingly.

"If you don't convey my heart-felt feelings to the Maharaja, how much hurt I will feel? Kaka! You can understand it very well. I hope that after Rama's message, you should convey my message also. It'll please me." Lakshmana smiled, looking at Rama.

"The boat is ready, Lord!" spoke Guha.

They all advanced towards the boat.

At the entrance of the boat, its owner was standing overbrimmed with emotions with his folded hands.

"He's the most skilled boatman of this area,

and his boat is considered to be most reliable. When the Ganga flows in full speed, all other boats fail to withstand her. Then his is the sole boat that carries all across the river. His style of rowing the boat is wonderful. His boat shows no fear of the river's waves but plays with them sportively." Guha looked at the boat's owner admiringly.

"Does this man bear any name or is he merely called a boatman?" asked Lakshmana mirthfully.

"Your servant is called 'Kevat' He folded his hands and touched his brow with them. He spoke in a pleasant voice, "I always used to think that if I'd done any noble deed in my life, I should be fortunate enough to have a 'darshan' of Shri Rama as a blessing. When I heard the news about the Lord's coronation, I'd a burning desire in me to go to the holy city of Ayodhya and make my life worth living by just having his glimpse from the distance."

"Did you receive this news from the palace?" Guha laughed.

"My boat floats upon the Ganga and I get the news of the world here itself on my boat. Whosoever goes across the Ganga brings domestic and foreign news with him," Kevat folded his hands.

"Then why didn't you come to Ayodhya city?" Lakshmana shot a sharp arrow of a question from the bow of his tongue.

"If it's a passionate desire, it can never go unfulfilled. It means that your desire didn't have the required intensity, otherwise you would have definitely come there."

"No, my desire was ardent. I'm ready to take an oath upon Mother Ganga." Kevat, after responding to Lakshmana, looked at Rama in the hope that he would say something. But Rama was enjoying this argument.

"Then what happened to your intense desire?"

"It's such a mystery that I'm still feeling it at present but I don't happen to understand it." Kevat's lips were trembling.

"You tell us about the mystery, O boatman! I've studied many scriptures these days by the grace of Rama. I'll unlock your mystery." Lakshmana felt that after so many days he had got a chance to make a game of someone.

"You are telling the truth that you're the only one who is worthy enough to solve this mystery. My sense of wisdom has become almost dead in an attempt to solve this riddle. Feeling exhausted, I've dropped the very idea of knowing the mystery. Only now I have got peace of mind." Raising his hands towards the sky, Kevat began to say, "When I learnt from the discussion of some traders in my boat that the next day had been fixed for Shri Rama's coronation, I fastened this new boat of mine to the bathing-steps and instructed my servants not to use the boat in any circumstances until I returned. I was just taking leave of my servants when a mendicant appeared before me and asked me to take him across the Ganga. Generally, I don't charge any money from saints if they use my boat. I think what difference it will make if I take five or ten saints in a gigantic boat of mine across the Ganga. I'm not much greedy of money. But to unfasten my grand boat just for one mendicant didn't appeal to my practical wisdom. I told that mendicant that I was in a hurry to go somewhere else and so he should request some other boatman. Moreover, the sun was going to set and I had already anchored my boat to the ghat. Now it would be rowed next morning. Then that mendicant smilingly asked me how the sunset or the sunrise was connected with the boat. He said, 'Does the Ganga stop flowing thinking that the sun has set?'

I liked his reasoning, but I couldn't digest it. I asked him why he didn't go by a small boat carrying four or five persons. Then that mendicant told me that nobody was interested in carrying him across the Ganga without money. At that time I felt irritated, taking him to be an obstacle in my way. I asked him if small boatmen were hesitant in carrying him across the Ganga, how he thought I, who was the owner of a very big boat meant for forty to fifty passengers, would unfasten the boat and carry him across the Ganga."

"Then what did that mendicant say to you?" Sumantra opened his mouth.

"He said, 'This suggestion has been given to me only by these small boatmen. They told me that if I wanted to go across the Ganga free of charge, I should go to the crazy Kevat who was under the influence of saints, and that he took many sadhus across the Ganga daily. At that time your boat was in the midst of the Ganga river. Then one devotee, just to help me, proposed to those boatmen that he would pay them as much money as they charged from one passenger. But the small boatmen said that they could think of carrying me across the river only when he paid as much money as they charged from ten passengers; they wouldn't row the boat at night for one passenger," The boatman looked at Sumantra and folded his hands. Then he looked at Lakshmana and said, "God knows how this much rudeness penetrated my voice to tell that mendicant that he must at least understand this much mathematical calculation that if those boatmen were so discourteous not to row their boat for him, how he could then row his ship-like boat for him."

“Did that mendicant go away then?” asked Lakshmana.

“No, he didn’t go. It seemed to me that he was like a ghost who had clung to me.” Kevat continued, “He asked me whether I would refuse to go across the Ganga if a group of fifty persons just came to me or if a very rich person offered me as much money as I would charge from a hundred passengers.”

“Then what was your reply?” There was curiosity in Sita’s eyes.

“Mother!” Kevat’s eyes were filled with tears and he felt choked. He spoke in his choked voice, “My sense told me to say to him that even if I was paid double the money I wouldn’t agree to go. But Mother Ganga checked me from telling the untruth. I told him that I would then unfasten my boat and take them across the Ganga. That mendicant upon this then said , ‘It means that in your eyes there is more importance of money than of faith or religion.’ I said, ‘No, I’m the adorer of faith, not of money and I’m getting ready to go somewhere on a noble mission.’ At this, that mendicant asked me whether I wouldn't have got delayed for that place to go to in case I had taken anybody across the Ganga out of lust for double money. Then I replied that in that case I would have reached the holy place quite conveniently by means of a speedy chariot after earning more money. I continued, 'I've built my new boat recently and so my eyes are fixed upon money, otherwise my happiness of life lies in faith, and not in money."

"What happened thereafter?" asked Guha.

"O Nishadraja!" Kevat bowed his head before Guha, "I was then in a fix. On one side was the keen desire of contenting myself with Shri Rama's *darshan* in Ayodhya and on the other side was the persistence of this mendicant to take him across the Ganga. He said that it was obligatory for him to go across the Ganga. That if I didn't want to take him in his boat across the river, he would swim across it, but he would never return to those boatmen and request them again. My servants then said, 'You should not fall into the trap of this hypocrite mendicant. Even the most skilled swimmer can't think of crossing this fast flowing Ganga.

If somebody steps into the furious Ganga, it means directly to commit suicide. Either the whirlpool of the Ganga will swallow him or the crocodiles of the river will make a dinner of him. I told that mendicant to take rest at night at my house and as soon as the day dawned, he would be taken in a small boat across the river. But he was a senseless, illogical mendicant. He listened to me and smilingly said, 'It seems that I'm being summoned by the Ganga.' Saying so, he marched forward speedily towards the banks of the Ganges and said, 'Mother, I'm coming. It's only you who will take me across.' This brought my heart to my mouth. I felt that if I didn't stop him, he would jump into the Ganga and then I would hold myself responsible for his untimely death."

"How can you say that that mendicant would definitely die," asked Lakshmana.

"Because the flow of its water was so terrible that even my gigantic boat, only if rowed skillfully by many rowers, could reach the bank safely. In such a state, a person would be carried away like a straw," said Kevat.

"Then what did you say?" asked Guha.

"I prevented him by shouting at him and said, 'Stop, please. Why are you bent upon making my destiny a hell? Come back. I'm going to unfasten my boat.' He came back and seated himself in the boat, quite pleased as if he had paid me a hundred times more, and not just the double money, to take him across the Ganga. My helpers again put in their labour to untie it. They complained to me that it was my stupidity to suffer so much untimely loss for a crazy mendicant."

"Then why didn't you listen to them?" asked Lakshmana. "They were actually right to say so. After all, the boat was to be rowed by them. You were only to sit in the boat as a chief boatman and its owner."

"Yes, this is what all happened. As long as that mendicant was in my boat sailing on the Ganga, he went on reciting Vedic hymns."

"How did you then come to know that those were Vedic hymns?" Lakshmana cornered Kevat.

"What do I know whether those were Vedic hymns? I did not understand their meanings, but I was experiencing tranquility of mind caused by the sound of those words. After singing two psalms when that mendicant paused and looked at me smilingly, I asked him what language they were written in. Then he was the one who told me that he was reciting aromatic Vedic hymns by the grace of God. It took my rowers double the time to reach the ghat as they had to tackle the stormy waves of the Ganga. When our boat touched the ghat, I said to him, 'Do you know what ungood you've done to me? You've done a great injustice to me by saying that you're going to jump into the Ganga. Never do such a thing to anyone in future.' The mendicant spoke: 'If I'd said the same thing to other rowers, they wouldn't have even turned to look at me. So, it makes no difference to anyone.' He glanced at me with his mystic eyes and said, 'If I'd jumped into the Ganga, it wouldn't have affected your occupation.'

"Then what did you say?" smiled Sita.

"I said, 'I don't know whether it would

have affected my work or not. But this much I know that it would certainly have left a bad mark upon my soul. It would have perished under the weight of my consciousness of sin.' Then the mendicant asked me what that noble deed was for which I was so much anxious. I told him that I was going to attend Shri Rama's coronation ceremony and gratify myself with his *darshan* in the auspicious procession. I told him it was he who had created obstacles in my way. Actually, I never talk with any mendicant in this rude way. But that day I said everything that I could say to that mendicant to pour out my anger and anguish by way of remonstration. There was a current of reproach in my voice. I was making him realise that he had been violent to me. The only difference is that he employed the weapon of religion for violence without using any other weapon as a prop. If anybody had ordered him at the sword point to take him across the Ganga, he would have to do. That mendicant compelled me to take him across the Ganga at the sword-point." Kevat paused for a while as if he had found himself transported to that time.

"Whatever I say to anyone, all people take it ill. This question of mine may hurt you, but I'm requesting you to excuse me from it as it is out of curiosity I'm asking you." Lakshmana took an advantage of Kevat's short silence and tried to corner him, using his gift of the gab. Since then Lakshmana was wiggling out of pain that he couldn't entrap the ordinary boatman in the net of his gift of the gab. He looked at Rama. Rama was already looking at him. His eyes charged with mysterious rays seemed to have studied Lakshmana. They were telling him that howsoever he might try to corner the truth, it couldn't be. Only the doer was besieged by the attraction of truth. Truth is always extraordinary even if it is possessed by an ordinary and ignorant person; if the precious stones are in the hands of a poor man, their value doesn't diminish. Lakshmana fixed his eyes upon the boatman and making his voice stronger asked, "Was any other boatman from Shringverpura's Ganga going to Ayodhya to catch a sight of Shri Rama? Why were you alone so much interested in Shri Rama? You have never had any introduction with him? If it had been said by Nishadraja Guha, we could have understood it because Shri Rama looks upon him as his friend. In other words, I would like to know why you wanted to leave your work just to catch a glimpse of Shri Rama from a distance. It was not that mendicant who was impractical in behaviour but you."

Except Rama's, everyone else's face was conveying the feeling that Lakshmana had been cruel to him more than expected. It was just like hurting one's feelings.

All were astonished to see that Lakshmana's words didn't hurt Kevat at all. Instead, he smiled and looked at Lakshmana, amazed. He folded his hands with full devotion before Lakshmana and said, "My Lord! You're the younger brother of the omniscient and so you're also All-knowing. At that time that mendicant had also asked me the same question. He said, 'What lies in Rama that though you're a stranger to him, you are ready to go to Ayodhya just to catch a glimpse of him?' And the same question you've asked me."

"Then what was your reply, O Kevat?" asked Sita while looking at Lakshmana.

Lakshmana looked at Sita. Her smile was telling him that he had to bow down.

"I said, 'Once a convoy of twenty to fifty sages was sitting in my boat. They were talking about Shri Rama. Seven *Rishis* out of them were saying that Shri Rama is nobody else but the incarnation of Lord Vishnu. Then other rishis didn't agree with them. They said that they consider Rama only a king's son. Then those rishis said that they must understand that after seeing the holy character of the prince, Lord Vishnu had enshrined himself in the present Shri Rama after bidding good-bye to the Latex Sea. Even then other rishis didn't share the views of the seven rishis. Till the end of their talk they remained stuck to their words saying that Shri Rama is only a well-cultured prince. But then I saw a light between my two eyes and in it I saw the image of Lord Vishnu. He was equipped with his bow and arrows. I thought that the prince of Ayodhya, Shri Rama must be a person par excellence. Since then my soul became thirsty of catching a sight of Shri Rama, only his *darshan*."

"Then why didn't you come to Ayodhya? Why did you ignore your inner voice? Why did you rob yourself of seeing Living God? What happened to your burning desire?" It seemed that when Lakshmana saw that every unmistakable assault of his was going waste, he felt bewildered. To know Rama's reaction Lakshmana looked towards Rama. Rama was already looking at Lakshmana. Rama's voice was echoing in Lakshmana's heart that he would cut a sorry figure.

"After hearing the mystic words of that mendicant, the tide of my longing ebbed down on the wait dam?" It looked as if Kevat were in hypnosis.

"What did that mendicant say?" asked Sumantra, peering through his aged eyes dilated with awe.

"While standing at his own place, it seemed as if he looked around in all directions; he stared at me with his profound, mystic eyes and said as if he were blessing me, 'Go and enjoy yourself, O boatman! You needn't go to Ayodhya. Wait patiently, Ayodhya will itself approach you. Intensify your thirst; the rain-bearing clouds will be obliged to come to you. Solidify your wait. To go across the Ganga Shri Rama will step into this very boat which you have used to take me across, and will gratify you. You shouldn't miss the chance then. Earn as much as you want. Remember, don't let the time slip out of your hand. Beg of him as much as you wish. Such golden opportunities are very rare. I've paid my own fare. He'll pay his own, take it from him.' "

Lakshmana felt he didn't even come to know when and who clipped his wings when he was flying on the wings of vanity in the sky. He realised this only when he fell from the sky upon his face on the dusty earth.

"Lakshmana!" spoke Rama softly, "Come out of your thoughts and help Sita board the boat."

"One request, Lord!" Kevat stood before Rama with his bowed head.

"Speak out."

"It is said by our sages and thinkers that if any guest comes to one's door, he should be treated like God. I want this privilege to wash God's feet."

In reply, Rama simply smiled.

Taking it to be Rama's consent, Kevat had already gestured for the ingredients required for washing his feet. His assistants at once put a stool for Rama to sit on. His son kept a wash bowl and his wife started pouring Ganga water from the copper-urn. Charged with emotion Kevat began to wash Rama's feet.

Guha thought why it didn't strike him. Then he felt that since Shri Rama hailed him as his friend, he had begun to think himself to be at par with him. Here he missed the chance and that emotional boatman, calling himself the servant of Rama, got all that which is difficult even for gods and sages to get.

Kevat put Rama's feet in his lap and wiped them with his stole softly and carefully. At this juncture of departure only Guha received

SHASHI

special permission to be in the boat, and that too only up to the other ghat. After bidding adieu to Shri Rama across Ganga, he was to return in the same boat.

The boat set out. Sumantra, the family of Guha and his officials accorded Shri Rama an emotional see-off.

All were sitting quietly in the boat. Lakshmana and Guha were looking at Kevat who was sitting at the feet of Rama. His very mouth was expressing that something very sweet was being eaten by him.

"O Kevat!" Guha cried, "Why are you sitting on the land like this? It doesn't look nice."

"O Nishadraja! Where is the land? This boat itself is my mother. I'm sitting in the lap of my mother and that mother of mine is in the lap of Mother Ganga, the Mother of the Earth. Even otherwise we, the rowers, are in the habit of sitting on the ground."

"Why don't you speak the truth, O boatman? Tell Nishadraja that you're tempted to sit at Shri Rama's feet," smiled Lakshmana.

"Leave something unsaid, Lakshmanaji!" spoke Kevat.

The boat was now in the midst of 'Bhagirathi.' Looking at the Ganga, Sita greeted her with her folded hands. Admiringly she said, "Goddess Gange! The wisest and noblest son of Maharaja Dashratha is going to fulfill his vow. Bless him to return Ayodhya safe and sound with me and his younger brother after fulfilling his vow. On their safe return, I'll give cows in charity and offer my prayer to gods in temples, at pilgrimages situated on your banks."

Sita kept on praying to the Ganga and all others thought it better to keep quiet so that there might not be any interruption in her worship.

The boat touched the ghat. All stepped down the boat.

Kevat with his folded hands stood before Rama.

"O Kevat! I've also nothing to pay you," smiled Rama.

"O Kevat! Take the fruit of your labour," Sita

stretched her hand with an ornament towards him. "Definitely, it will be more than your expectations."

"No, Mother goddess! This is not even an atom of what I wish for," the boatman folded his hands, "The mendicant had told me not to miss the chance."

A nasty thought came into the furious mind of Lakshmana to ask him whether the sum and substance of his whole story was to take the price of the whole boat instead of the fare to take them across the Ganga. He doesn't know that he is not only putting Shri Rama in a great fix but also disrespecting him. Destiny is also playing its weird role. Shri Rama, who can pay him the value of such countless boats, is now standing as a poor man before an ordinary boatman. Lakshmana thought that his wrath would make him weep. But he said nothing. He guided his angry mind to watch the events occurring silently. He shouldn't wreak his fury on an incomplete incident. He had already suffered from punishment a little while ago because of this reason.

Sita put her hand into the pouch to take out some more ornaments.

"O Lord! I don't want any gold."

"Then what do you want?" asked Rama smilingly and softly.

"Only the exchange value. There is no system of using money in our society of boatmen. It's the barter system that exists. A farmer in exchange of his grain accepts only the required things from ironsmiths, potters or goldsmiths. In the same way, we also do the same."

"Speak clearly what you've in your mind, Kevat!" Guha intervened.

"I don't know whether you are an incarnation or not. I had simply heard the talk of sages and on the same ground I take you to be so. We worship even trees and stones, feeling that God exists in them. Our heart accepts it. My soul also accepts you as the incarnation of God and I request you with the same feeling to come to my ghat. With the help of this boat of mine, you crossed the Ganga. A day will definitely come when all, after their demise, will come to your door-step i.e. your ghat. At that time, O my Pilot, don't forget this servant of yours and take me across the bar. Nobody else but you can help me get the fruit of my labour." An ocean of tears gushed out of Kevat's eyes and he lay down on Rama's feet.

Rama bent to lift him. He pressed both of his arms lovingly and gently. Lowering his eye lashes, he gave his assent by way of smiling.

The wrathful mind of Lakshmana shrieked : What's all this? Is Rama the incarnation? If not, why did he share Kevat's feelings? Why didn't he say even once that he was not the incarnation? Why didn't he tell Kevat that he was only a prince discarded by his father? If he was really the incarnation, he should prove it.

The discretion of Lakshmana smiled : 'If you keep quiet for some time, I'll be able to understand something. At the initial stage of every talk, you begin to commit mistakes. After that you seek facts to prove them wrong. It is due to your prejudice that my sense becomes the victim of suspicion. After today I'll not react immediately under the impact of your advice.

I'll first witness the entire episode patiently and then arrive at the conclusion.'

The boat retreated on its journey. Gazing fascinatingly at the Ganga banks as if it were a point, and distracting the attention of Kevat, Guha said in his heart-touching voice, "O boatman! You're very shrewd. On the one hand, you've enhanced the honour of boatmen and on the other hand, you've earned something that will let you enter not only this world but also the other world as a conqueror. It's truly said that the company of mendicants enables a person to reach the summit of his life."